I0820387

HAUNTED
FLORIDA KEYS

ELIZABETH RANDALL AND WILLIAM R. RANDALL JR.

Published by Haunted America
A division of The History Press
An imprint of Arcadia Publishing
Charleston, SC
www.historypress.com

All photos by William "Bob" Randall unless otherwise noted.
Front cover: The Artist House on Eaton Street in Key West is a bed-and-breakfast inn and the former home of Robert Gene Otto and his notorious Chucky-type companion, Robert.

First published 2026

Manufactured in the United States

ISBN 9781467159111
Hardcover ISBN 9781540299697

Library of Congress Control Number applied for.

Notice: The information in this book is true and complete to the best of our knowledge. It is offered without guarantee on the part of the author or The History Press. The author and The History Press disclaim all liability in connection with the use of this book.

Cigar maker, frond lady,
iguana man, voodoo chief,
live on a coquina raft,
the mast
is Bone Key.
—Author unknown

This book is dedicated,
with apologies,
to Robert the Doll.

CONTENTS

Acknowledgements

Thank you to all the past and present visitors and residents of Key West who supplied the quotes for each haunted site. Thanks to our commissioning editor at The History Press, Chad Rhoad; the staff at the Casa Marina; Pete at the Seashell Motel; the Ghosts & Graveyards haunted tour; Judy Blume for her help displaying the works of local authors via Books & Books; Faith Price, branch manager of the Pine Key library; the Key Largo library for carrying the rare book *The Florida Keys: A History Through Maps*; Sue Burke, executive assistant to Mayor Jim Scholl; Connie Kingdom at Cheeca Lodge; Tony Tarracino (RIP), whom I (Liz) interviewed in the 1970s; and most of all to Tennessee Williams, whose literary genius inspired me to move to the Keys, where his ghost, I fervently hope, still resides.

Prologue

Should we have stayed at home wherever that might be?
—Elizabeth Bishop

The first time I (Liz) saw the Florida Keys was from the window of a Greyhound bus. US 1 went north and south, and by the time we lumbered into the Keys, the road was two lanes flanked by canals and mangroves. From time to time I spotted someone fishing, wearing rubber boots up to the knees.

This was better than the view as the bus lurched through the violent surges of traffic in Miami, Cutler Ridge, and Homestead. Cars were lined up at all the gas stations. It was the middle of the gas wars, and in 1978, the price of fuel was as high as one dollar per gallon. I was on the bus because I couldn't afford to go by car, and besides, I drove a 1968 Vega, a vehicle basically held together by rust molecules and clearly ill-equipped to navigate the eighteen-mile stretch—more than once, anyway.

I was going to the Keys to apply for the position of home economics teacher at Coral Shores High School. Mike Lannon, the principal, was going to pick me up at the bus stop in Tavernier, which was also a Dairy Queen. The school was ten miles farther south.

It would make a more interesting story if Mike interviewed me at the Dairy Queen over Blizzards. Instead, we drove to the high school, where he ushered me into his office. During the interview, he revealed a ruse he used to disarm applicants. When I sat down across from his desk, the arm of my chair fell off. I gasped, and Mike smiled smugly.

Later in the interview, Mike confessed that he never got the chair fixed because when the arm fell off, it told him how the person in front of him reacted to the unexpected. Did he blame the chair? Apologize? Try to fix it? Curse? Or did he carry on smoothly and confidently?

A lot of unexpected things happen when you're a high school teacher. But that's a whole other book. Mike Lannon was only seven years older than me, and he would go on to become the superintendent of education for Monroe County. That was one unexpected thing. The other was that despite my dismal broken chair response, Mike must have been pretty desperate, because I passed his test. He said the job was mine because I was young and "hungry"—which must have been a reference to my teacher's salary, which was guaranteed to keep me that way. My first teaching job was in the Florida Keys! It was great, even though my Vega totally rusted out within a month.

I taught at Coral Shores for two years. During the spring of my first year, in 1980, several of my students disappeared for weeks. It turned out they accompanied their fathers in boats for the lucrative business of transporting Cubans to Florida after Castro opened the prisons for that purpose. For months, yellow school buses delivered these refugees to the Krome booking facility in Homestead. No one could enter or leave the Keys without a full accounting of his or her birthplace. This hurt tourism and so enraged the locals that they tried to secede from the United States by forming the Conch Republic. Their flag was blue with a conch shell in the center of a fiery sun. It's still displayed everywhere.

As mentioned, my car was not a reliable vehicle, so I stayed put. Tavernier was a town whose entertainment consisted of clogging to bluegrass music and a bit of banjo playing. It was quiet, almost respectable. There were chickens scratching and roosters crowing. Even though the bars started serving at nine o'clock in the morning, the Upper Keys were different from Key West, whose antics ranged from rowdy bar scenes to all-out nudity at Fantasy Fest.

When I quit teaching to work at a local newspaper, the *Conch Shell*, I went to Key West often and to all the Keys in between for stories. The pay was even worse than teaching, but I loved the job, which entailed everything from selling ads to writing articles and taking pictures (developed in a darkroom). To get stories, I did things like deep sea fishing (so seasick), lobster trapping, shark catching, and interviewing people like Lawton Chiles when he was governor. On Duck Key, I covered a beauty contest for the Toppers Club, an elite organization that admitted no members under six feet tall. (I'm five three.)

The Conch Republic flag.

Regarding ghost sightings, I discovered such things cannot be planned. Ghost tours may give you the history of ghostly visits, but such events are random and unpredictable, if they occur at all. Trying to conjure spirits is futile. You see them when they want you to see them.

It was at No Name Key, in the Lower Keys, that I saw the ghost. No Name Key is about thirty miles from Key West, a quaint Key, noteworthy in those days for the telephone lines, which stopped at the No Name Pub right before the bridge. There was no electricity on No Name Key, and residents used generators and solar power. Where the telephone lines stopped, it was easy to imagine you were walking into an earlier time.

I was doing just that, walking over the bridge through the broiling heat—the kind of high temperatures that make cartoon thermometers explode—when I saw a man at the end of the bridge under a shady hammock, waving his hands. The man had a white beard and wore suspenders and a broad-brimmed hat low on his head. There were work boots on his feet. I shielded my eyes from the sun, blinked, and he became transparent. Then he was gone. According to local lore, apparitions in remote areas of hardwood forest are fairly common. It could have been the No Name Hermit, who is discussed in one of the chapters on the Lower Keys.

Eventually, I left the Keys, but it was hard to do. I loved Tavernier, a sparsely populated Key in those days. I loved the lifestyle, which had to do with boats and fishing, tiki huts, harbors, bluegrass and reggae music. Long pants were considered formal wear. The first movie theater and McDonalds didn't go up until I'd lived there a year. As a teacher and a news reporter, I knew most of the people in town. But there were no real opportunities for me, and I didn't want to hang out in a small school or a sparse office on a small island in the middle of the ocean for the rest of my life. I was young, and it was time to see the rest of the world.

I moved to the mainland, but I went back to the Keys often and took my family. The Keys were part of my husband Bob's past as well. An air force brat, he lived in Cutler Ridge as a teen, and he and his brother, Al, fished all up and down the Keys. Their best day was at the Cut in Key Largo. Bob put a shrimp on a hook, threw it in the water, and came up with a twelve- to fourteen-inch snapper. Al did the same and caught a snapper. Bob put half a shrimp on the hook, threw it in the water, and came up with another snapper. He tried a fourth of a shrimp, and it worked just as well. Al and Bob caught forty snappers that day. They had a fish fry outdoors at a friend's house in Islamorada close to Holiday Isle.

At the fish fry, Bob noticed a man who kept reappearing in the line. He looked soaking wet, and he never carried a plate. It wasn't until the Key lime pie was served that he literally disappeared: there one minute, gone the next. No one knew who he was; there was no trace of him. Some of the resident Conchs speculated that he was a drowned specter from the 1935 Labor Day hurricane. They said they'd seen such apparitions before.

These experiences on those strips of coral and limestone gave us the idea for *Haunted Florida Keys.* Bob and I work as a photojournalist team, and we have written eight books, including *Haunted St. Augustine and St. Johns County* and *Women in White*. With our knowledge of the Keys and Key West, we made it our goal to present the haunting beauty, and the haunts, of one of our preferred and well-traveled destinations.

We hope you, our reader, enjoy the book and visit some of our favorite spooky places.

Liz and Bob

Introduction
A Brief History of the Keys and Key West

I don't care what anybody says about me as long as it isn't true.
—*Truman Capote*

Key West is one of the reliable spots in the United States for supernatural sightings; there is even a Ghostbusters type of business called the Conch Republic Investigative Paranormal Team. One reason for the city's spooky distinction is that Key West is old—the oldest city in South Florida. The land is even older. Millions of years ago, the Key islands were under water. Tens of thousands of years ago, when the waters receded, all of the Keys were connected to the Florida mainland. Eventually, the waters rose again, trapping wildlife on emerging islands.

These exquisite atolls, the Florida Keys, belonged to Native American tribes dating back to AD 800. European visitors to the islands date back to the fourteenth and fifteenth centuries. The Portuguese put the Keys on a map in the early sixteenth century, and the Spaniards arrived a decade later looking for land and potable water.

Instead of water, the Spaniards found a rocky beachhead littered with human bones. No one knows if the bones represented a ritual burial based on religious beliefs or if the island was a dumping ground for bodies. Perhaps the beach was the site of a tribal war. It is known that Native American Indians, the first settlers in the Keys, were fierce, feared enslavement, and consequently slaughtered Spanish and English survivors of shipwrecks. In fact, in the 1800s, European settlers, aided by rival tribes, sold many of the Indians into slavery. By then, not many were left. The Spanish and English brought pestilence, flu, measles, and smallpox, which also ravaged Indian communities.

The Spanish never really settled in Key West, using it primarily as a salvage camp. In fact, the Keys were probably too rugged and primitive altogether for the Spanish conquistadors. The reef (a network of living coral nodules) that runs along the coastline was lethal to vessels, looming without warning, yet the Spanish didn't try to mark the reefs for passing ships. So when they were blown off course by storms, their hulls were torn apart by the rocky reef, and the vessels were lost to the owner. There were local lookouts for wrecked ships, and the first person to reach it took the lion's share of the booty. It was like legal piracy. In fact, wrecking was the Keys' first industry. It turned Key West into the wealthiest and most populated city in Florida. The last wrecking license was issued in 1921, but wrecking was really over by 1855.

Lighthouses (enabling captains to see at night) and steamships (less apt to be blown onto the reefs) caused wrecking as an occupation to dwindle. Lawlessness, yellow fever, hurricanes, fire, and the Seminole Indian Wars left the Florida Keys and Key West populated by only the hardiest of Conchs (native Key Westers), soldiers, wreckers, Bahamians, spongers, and Cuban cigar makers. As Spain's fortunes had declined, so had Florida's. By the time the Civil War and Reconstruction rolled around, in the 1860s, fewer than 3,000 people lived on the southernmost island. The rest of the Keys had barely 150 inhabitants altogether. Captured Confederate ships, trying to get cotton and other goods out of Southern harbors, comprised the only swag Union-occupied Key Westers picked up.

The coming of rail changed all that. Some of the Keys were created during the manufacture of Henry Flagler's Overseas Railroad, and some were joined with dredged fill dirt instead of bridges. The land between the bridges was muck, needing tons of soil and rocks. The completed bridges helped open Key West to tourist travel. Later, communities of homes, and their development—a practical move in the eyes of settlers—also altered the shape of the original limestone islands.

Yet practicality has nothing to do with living in or visiting the Keys. Romance draws people to the Keys and Key West. These isles survive in a remote area of the United States, a place as beautiful as it is mysterious. It is a romance that is humid, sensual, and reckless. A unique place haunted by its own turbulent history, the Keys are different from the black magic of New Orleans, different from the dreamy ambiance of Paris, different even

Above: A view of the Atlantic Ocean.

Right: Statue of Albert Kee, a Conch-blowing greeter.

Above: Sunset in Key Largo.

Opposite: A fighter jet zooms across a Key West sky.

today from the charm of the glittering Atlantic shore and Biscayne Bay, where people stay in tottering condominium towers because the view is so beautiful.

Instead, the Keys are composed of thousands of islands off the southern coast of Florida (forty-three are connected by bridges) and possessor of a living coral barrier reef, unique in the continental United States. The rocky shoreline that, as mentioned, routinely gored seagoing vessels before the advent of lighthouses, was just one of the risks associated with living or trading there.

The Keys are, after all, just a low-lying succession of coral and limestone clumps where the vast Atlantic Ocean meets the Gulf of Mexico, a frequent route of hurricanes. Danger has always been part of this southernmost attraction. It is not uncommon to see and hear navy aircraft roaring overhead from the Boca Chica training facility for combat aircraft.

Yet Key West is, ultimately, a Florida tourist city with only one airport and limited resources if you need to get out of town in a hurry (like during the advent of a hurricane). Summers in Key West, only ninety-five miles from Cuba, are sweltering and prone to hurricanes. Its sunsets are bloodred and splattered across the sky. There is a sense of living in the present, like in Las Vegas, but instead of neon and city lights a distinctly tropical setting with a blend of Caribbean, Cuban, and Bahamian colors and accents. There is a sense of the past as well, during rare occasions when the streets are deserted, and locals swear the ghost of William Faulkner walks his pet goat down Duval Street.

Sunset in the southernmost city.

There's the scent of magnolia wafting from tiki huts, boat parties, walks along the shore with sand between your toes and a sprig of frangipani in your hair. This is a city with no fear of darkness. Its people celebrate the sun going down at Mallory Square every night.

Key West International: Welcome to the Conch Republic!

In the past, Key West's geographic location was a lookout to thwart piracy. Its deep harbor advanced shipping in the Gulf of Mexico—yet survival was dicey. Disease was endemic on the ancient island. Yellow fever was transmitted by incoming and outgoing shipments. The disease hit Key West hard in the mid-nineteenth century, further decimating the population. There was also rampant typhoid and tuberculosis.

It was not easy in those days to live to a ripe old age on the Rock. And with death came the ghost stories. The ghosts of Key West embody its colorful past and teach quite a bit about history. In fact, you could say the ghosts of the Florida Keys are a metaphor for history. Bizarrely, ghosts are one way to keep the memories of Key West and the Florida Keys alive.

CHAPTER 1
HOMESTEAD

FLAMINGO IN THE EVERGLADES

I used to hunt plume birds, but since the game laws were passed, I have not killed a plume bird. For it is a cruel and hard calling not withstanding being unlawful. I make this statement upon honor.
—Guy Bradley in a letter to William Dutcher, head of the Audubon Society, around 1900

GHOST STORY

Guy Bradley was an unlikely prospect for a game warden in the Florida Everglades. A Yankee, Bradley migrated to South Florida, where he hunted birds for their plumes like everyone else. As the bird species—egrets, crane, stork, heron, spoonbill, etc.—began a quick march toward extinction, Bradley had a change of heart. He became a game warden and was deputized in Monroe County in 1902. Now the shoe was truly on the other foot, expressly in the Monroe County Everglades village called Flamingo, where Bradley declared war on poaching.

Flamingo's economy may have rested on its ability to market feathers. Bradley cared about the law and saving wildlife. Because he was passionate about protecting the remaining wild bird species, Bradley was good at his job. Maybe too good. In 1905, he came upon a father and two sons poaching egrets in the Everglades. Bradley warned them to stop. They argued. The elder poacher pulled out a rifle and shot the game warden dead.

The exact spot of Bradley's murder on Oyster Bay is marked with a roundish coquina monument outside the Guy Bradley Visitor Center. A few times a year, when the moon is full, locals fancifully claim to see the shadowy figure of Bradley standing guard. The National Fish and Wildlife Foundation annually celebrates one game warden's conservation creds with the Guy Bradley Award. This may explain why the shadows of birds, perhaps thousands of them, are reflected passing in silhouette above a flamingo moon on the nights the Guy Bradley apparition appears.

Bradley became known as the first martyr to environmentalism, and plume hunting was outlawed in Florida the year he died.

History

Located on the southernmost tip of the Everglades, Flamingo is one of Monroe County's haunted places, haunted by birds in particular. Founded in 1892, the remote location was named for the flamingos that once flocked on this spot. Around the turn of the twentieth century, Flamingo was heavily involved in the business of plume hunting, and poachers abounded. They decimated the flamingo population, and other bird species, for their feathers. Florida has always been a little like the Wild West, and Guy Bradley was not the first or the last game warden to die at the end of a poacher's rifle.

Flamingo was a small village. It was a place to fish and get away from it all. It was a place to view wildlife, including crocodiles and manatees. It was also a place for poachers to kill birds for their feathers, which were used primarily for ladies' hats. Like the wreckers farther south, hoping for a shipwreck, the poachers needed wild game, and they needed it while the fad was still afoot (or ahead, as the case may be). When the practice of slaughtering millions of birds for their plumage began to show its effects in decimated species, the practice was outlawed, around 1905. The village of Flamingo went into immediate decline. By the 1940s, Flamingo was considered a literal ghost town.

Today, what is left of Flamingo includes the Guy Bradley Visitor Center, a pink building, recently renovated and prone to educational displays in its gift shop. There is the park and the Flamingo Lodge. There is an old wooden amphitheater near a hiking trail where hordes of bloodsucking mosquitoes lie in wait.

A monument to Guy Bradley in the Everglades at the visitor center and trail.

The old wooden amphitheater near the hiking trail.

Flamingo is far from finished as a bird haven and rookery. The Audubon Society published a sighting of a flock of flamingos in the Everglades recently, arousing hope that the pink birds are back. Birds often brazenly assemble at low tide in front of the visitor center. Perhaps they celebrate their victory over feather rustlers and remind us to respect their lives.

ADDRESS:
EVERGLADES NATIONAL PARK/FLAMINGO VISITOR CENTER
1 FLAMINGO LODGE HIGHWAY, HOMESTEAD, FLORIDA

....

ALABAMA JACKS

I bought the place first as more or less a party place,
a place to entertain our friends.
—Jack Stratum, original owner

GHOST STORY

Alabama Jacks is on Card Sound, a two-lane road that just squeaks into Monroe County and eventually joins up to the Overseas Highway and North Key Largo. The bar is near the Crocodile Lake National Wildlife Refuge and a large Key Largo hammock. It used to be a deserted rail station and a fishing community with boats queuing the waterfront for a quarter of a mosquito-filled mile. Today, the mangrove-lined region hosts revelers and a few Card Sound ghosts.

The Labor Day hurricane of 1935 wiped out the Card Sound road (before it was named) and the World War I vets who worked it. A waiter at the bar reported a crew of men sitting around one of the square metal tables, dressed in bib overalls, felt caps, and brogans. He went to get some menus, and when he returned, the men were gone. "The funny thing is," he said, "they were all soaking wet. There were puddles on and around the chairs after the men disappeared."

Card Sound Road also had its share of tragedy. The demise of crash victims is another factor in the bar's eerie ambiance. In 2019, police warned

Alabama Jacks on Card Sound Road.

drivers of a suspicious man trying to stop cars in front of Alabama Jacks, a man who waved a flashlight and yelled. One driver who stopped to help said the man hopped into his car and then hopped out, leaving bloodstains on the seat. The Good Samaritan was so concerned that he pulled into the dirt parking lot amid the motorcycles and trucks of a weekend bar crowd. But the man was gone, vanished into the twilight. Paranormal buffs speculate that the man was the spirit of a recent boat crash victim near the Card Sound bridge.

History

Jack Stratum was dubbed Alabama Jack by a construction foreman who mistook the Georgia native's Southern drawl for that of an adjacent state. Jack started the bar in the 1950s when only one hundred people lived there. His wife, Alice, was famous for her crab cakes, and Jack had a pet racoon named Connie. Alabama Jack's tenaciousness was legend in the Keys.

It all began when he worked up north, where the money was, and started taking fishing vacations in the Keys. Jack came back every year. Eventually he bought the small abandoned building on Card Sound, which miraculously survived hurricanes. He put it on pilings, built a dock, and the rest is history.

Hurricanes swept the building off its pilings more than once. Jack rebuilt, even though at one point he was left with only a couple of walls and the floor. He rebuilt with a bar on a barge, in keeping with the ubiquitous presence of ready alcohol at any Keys event. Eventually, however, age and upkeep forced Alabama Jack and Alice to sell out and move to Homestead. Jack died in 1977 and was buried near a channel marker.

Today, Alabama Jacks is an open-air dive bar bordering a river that turns into an ocean. Its clientele is a mix of tourists and locals from Ocean Reef and Hope Sound. Boats cruise by close to the outer perimeter, but you can't really hear the motors. Inside, the band plays very loud Jimmy Buffett music, featuring a keyboardist who looks like Albert Einstein.

There is definitely a Keys ambiance to Alabama Jacks, which means different strokes for different folks. Some of the patrons and waiters wear their hair in abundant braids in the Rasta style. There is a Trump/Vance sign on the door. Birds perch on the chairs. Patrons carrying helmets and leather jackets walk in and out. The old wooden rail station is surrounded by lush, green deciduous trees. Motorcycles pull up noisily. There is the rich smell of cigars, even in the open air. License plates and dollar bills are tacked to the supporting beams.

Wine is served in small plastic cups, and on Sundays, it's pretty crowded. There is conch on the menu, including Alabama Jack's famous conch fritters, the size of a waffle and thick as a sirloin—making up, perhaps, for the conch salad, which is just a taste served in a miniscule plastic container. Don't drink too much. There is always road construction, and traffic can be bad as you wait out the tourists to get from Card Sound to the Overseas Highway.

ADDRESS:
ALABAMA JACKS
58000 CARD SOUND ROAD, HOMESTEAD, FLORIDA
305 248 8741

....

CHAPTER 2
UPPER KEYS

THE CARIBBEAN CLUB

The Highways of America are built chiefly of politics,
whereas the proper material is crushed rock or concrete.
—*Carl G. Fisher*

GHOST STORY

The Caribbean Club opened toward the end of the Great Depression, boasting good food, hotel rooms, and a waterfront boat dock on Blackwater Sound available for a small fee. Its remote yet accessible location made it a haven for a rendezvous away from the mainland.

In 1955, during one such assignation, a fire began in a hotel room from a source that was never identified—probably an errant lit cigarette. The room was the site of an adulterous liaison between a Miami woman, Jo Selby, and a married doctor, Frank Bussey. Selby died from smoke inhalation, but the good doctor survived with injuries. His wife, an opera singer, arrived at the hospital to nurse him back to health, but the newspapers were full of the licentious nature of the tragic occurrence. It is not known what became of Dr. Bussey and his enraged spouse, although the event was the perfect backdrop for an inspired operatic libretto.

Above: The famous Caribbean Club, founded by Carl Fisher.

Left: Bogie greets guests at the Caribbean Club.

The Caribbean Club gave up its hotel status after that fiery tragedy, which destroyed the hotel and the kitchen. According to locals, Ms. Selby, on the other hand, never left the retro Keys room. Patrons and staff occasionally smell smoke around the anniversary of her demise, which occurred on March 18. One witness insists that a wraith in the shape of a woman emerges from the ghostly fumes, looking around urgently as though she is seeking some sort of exit. Just as quickly as she appears, she is gone. However, since this is the Keys, the bar opens at seven o'clock in the morning and stays open until "oneish" o'clock in the morning. Consequently, ghost sighting accounts by patrons should be taken with a margarita and several grains of salt.

HISTORY

The name of the Caribbean Club was inspired by Havana Club, a brand of Cuban rum popular in the 1930s. From the outdoor wooden deck, where graceful palm trees frame the beachfront, the rear view of the Caribbean Club seems more like the "old Keys" than the front. There are picnic tables and fire pits and deck chairs. The roof is lettered with the name of the bar, decorative dolphins perch on the eaves, and a flag waves in the breeze of the bay. The retro building composed of wooden siding and brick still boasts the best sunset view in the Keys. If someone drinks too much Key Lime Pie Rum Punch, he can park at the Club overnight for twenty dollars. Wednesday is karaoke night, and there is live music on the waterfront stage. Food trucks are open 11:00 a.m. to 9:30 p.m. every day except Monday.

Famous for "a few mood shots" filmed by John Huston and designed for the 1948 black-and-white movie *Key Largo*, the Caribbean Club was the last effort of an ailing and broke Carl Fisher, a developer also known as Mr. Miami Beach and the father of the modern highway system. He saw the club as a "poor man's fishing retreat," and its opening nearly coincided with his death in 1939, making it one of the oldest bars in the Florida Keys today.

Fisher is famous for roads. He led the attempt to build the transcontinental Lincoln Highway, which connected the East and West Coasts. After several failed efforts, he pushed forward the Indianapolis Motor Speedway, home of the yearly Indianapolis 500. He was perhaps the first proponent of US 1, the highway that ends in Key West.

A man with Mr. Magoo eyesight and a sixth-grade education, Fisher was known for his stunts as much as for his business prowess. Promoting a car dealership, he pushed a new car off the dealership roof (how did it get up there?) and then drove away in it. Fisher and a partner purchased the patent rights for acetylene-driven headlights. They founded a company, called Prest-O-Lite, which made them rich until electric headlights were invented. As prominent citizens, Fisher and his wife were featured often in the society pages of the *Key West Citizen* and the *Miami Herald*.

An entrepreneur of great imagination, Fisher was still capable of vanity and prejudice. As a wealthy white man in the post-Reconstruction era, Fisher observed Jim Crow laws and did not allow anyone who was not a White Anglo-Saxon Protestant into his hotels or bars. This was unintentionally reenacted in one of *Key Largo*'s exterior shots, when Edward G. Robinson's character locks the Indians out of the bar during a hurricane.

Sadly, this sort of prejudice was not unusual in the segregated South. In fact, Miami Beach, which Fisher created by building a barrier island in Biscayne Bay, did not allow Jewish doctors fleeing the Holocaust to work in their hospitals. So the Jewish doctors converted an old Carl Fisher hotel into their own hospital, Mount Sinai. A place of healing seems a fitting epilogue to a Fisher property.

Today, US 1, the Dixie Highway, is bumper-to-bumper outside the Caribbean Club on Sundays as tourists inch their way by car from a weekend of Keys-style partying to the mainland. The road, which Fisher championed, was controversial when it was first envisioned. The *Orlando Sentinel* came out against it in an editorial, but the Miamians were all for it. Historians speculate about whether the Keys would have advanced as a tourist destination without the asphalt artery to and from the Rock. Without Fisher, the Caribbean Club would be a fringe of mangroves instead of a vintage bar in the Florida Keys. While scarcely an improvement on nature, the club is historic, and it is here to stay.

Address:
The Caribbean Club
104080 Overseas Highway, Mile Marker 104, Bay Side
Key Largo, Florida
305 451 4466

....

THE LARGO SOUND ROCK CASTLE

It was as though I'd been to one of those supernatural castles visited by characters in legends: once away, you do not remember, all that is left is the ghostly echo of haunting wonder.
—Truman Capote

Ghost Story

Key Largo is Spanish for "long key" (not to be confused with the actual Long Key at mile marker 67.5), and the island features some of the highest ground in the Florida Keys. This becomes important during a hurricane on an island with an average land elevation of seven feet. In 1920, Dr. George Engel tempted fate to erect the home of his dreams on the ocean side of the Atlantic next to a six-foot-deep harbor. What possessed the New Jersey dentist to build a turreted coral rock castle on the brink of Largo Sound? And what did the eccentric choice cost him?

Dr. Engel lived in his castle until his death in 1945. Since then, the abode has been known as the Haunted House on the Largo Sound. Although the castle was not destroyed during the 1935 Labor Day hurricane thanks to

A view of the Key Largo Sound Rock castle and pickleball court.

its three-foot-thick walls, its survival was not without consequences. The entire lower floor of the castle flooded, and legend has it that the doctor's mother was alone during the storm and took refuge in one of the towers. The fifteen-foot storm surge beat the first-floor furniture against the thick walls with crashes and banging sounds. After the prolonged trauma, it is said, Mrs. Engel was institutionalized. It is also rumored that residents and passersby still hear the furniture banging around as though it were trying to break through the walls. The sound is loud and discomfiting and has never been satisfactorily explained.

History

The Key Largo Sound Coral Castle was only the second home constructed in Key Largo. Today it is still standing and occupying the same space on which it was originally built. A historic landmark as well as valuable real estate, the castle has nine rooms, four bathrooms, and over four thousand square feet of space.

Its address, 55 Oceana Drive in Key Largo, is not listed on the National Register of Historic Places. One of its former owners, a Mrs. Gautier, purchased the castle in 1952 and renovated the house by detaching the stone parapets from the roof, which rendered the abode ineligible for historic status. However, it is the oldest home still standing in Key Largo today.

Someone bought it in 2021 for $1.4 million, and in 2024, it was for sale again for almost $2.6 million. Shots of the interior are available on Zillow. The house is secluded, separated from the ocean by a seawall and surrounded by palm trees. There is a pickleball court adjacent to the deserted castle.

This historic Key Largo castle is not to be confused with the Coral Castle in Homestead, erected by Edward Leedskalnin. Claiming to know the secrets of the pyramids, Leedskalnin moved over one thousand tons of stone unaided. Unlike the privately owned castle in Key Largo, the limestone Homestead version is a museum and open to the public.

Address:
55 Oceana Drive, Mile Marker 103.5, Oceanside
Key Largo, Florida

. . . .

HURRICANE MEMORIAL: OCEANSIDE HURRICANE MONUMENT

Dedicated to the memory of the civilians and war veterans whose lives were lost in the hurricane of September second, 1935.
—Plaque on the hurricane monument

There are two hurricane memorials in the Upper Keys. Both honor the lives of men and women who died in the 1935 Labor Day hurricane.

Ghost Story

The Oceanside Hurricane Monument contains the ashes of around three hundred individuals, mostly World War I vets who drowned on that fateful day. Originally, the government wanted individual coffins for each victim, but this proved to be too time-consuming as the swampy heat of the Keys accelerated decomposition. Decaying bodies were found as far as Flamingo

The Oceanside Hurricane Monument in Islamorada.

in the Everglades, and recovery took over a year. Eventually, the bodies were gathered and burned and the ashes set aside. In 1937, these ashes were interred in the hurricane monument by Roosevelt's Works Progress Administration. Nearly five thousand people attended the dedication ceremony.

The monument is a salve to the shock and terror of that fateful long-ago Labor Day. Islamorada considers the monument an emblem of spirit and strength. Since the two-hundred-mile-an-hour winds tracked close to the hurricane monument ninety years ago, it is natural that some ghostly activity has ensued. However, this ghost story has more to do with weather patterns, appropriately enough.

If it's raining when you are visiting the hurricane monument, get an umbrella and stick around. The combination of clear skies and scattered rain makes it an ideal setting for viewing a rainbow. But it's not just any rainbow. More than one tourist or local has reported that after the rain, they saw a colorful arc bending over the hurricane monument and touching the mainland.

History

The hurricane monument is comprised of Keystone, which is a decorative type of fossilized coral and limestone that was quarried near Windley Key until the 1960s. The stone shaft of the monument is twelve feet tall. A graphic etching on the monument's face shows the effect of the roiling two-hundred-mile-per-hour winds characterizing the deadly hurricane's strength. Framed by palm trees, the hurricane memorial stands on a pedestal before a tiled mosaic of the Florida Keys. Lights are kept on all night, illuminating Islamorada's symbol of remembrance.

The Oceanside Hurricane Monument, also known as the Florida Keys Memorial, is listed on the National Register of Historic Places.

Address:
Oceanside Hurricane Monument
Mile Marker 81.6

....

HURRICANE MEMORIAL: BAYSIDE CHANNEL 2 PIERS

The veterans of World War I were promised a bonus but due to the Great Depression of the early 1930s the government was without funds. Roosevelt was president and formed the Florida Emergency Relief Administration to create jobs for those out of work.
On November 1934, the government sent 600 veterans to build bridges to replace the ferries. The main and largest camp was here.
On September 2, 1935, the great Labor Day Hurricane with 200 mile per hour winds and 20 foot waves destroyed the camp and the railway. The road was rebuilt on the railway bridges leaving the unfinished piers as a memorial to the hundreds who lost their lives.
—Plaque at the site

Ghost Story

Located on the bay side, these are the original pylons the World War I vets built. Late at night, there is almost no one in the vicinity. But were you there, you might hear the voices of men laughing and playing cards. More than one person has relayed hearing such sounds along with the faint murmur of a radio and a rushing sound like wind or waves.

The highway bridge piers memorializing the veterans who built them.

A visitor to a public bathroom on Madeira Road, near the site, reported that the locked door reverberated with a steady pounding, like someone wanting in. When the man opened the door, no one was there. Other people have reported similar stories. It is commonly believed that the pounding is from the hurricane dead, trying to escape the storm.

History

Begun in 1934, the concrete piers were, of course, never finished because the men who worked on them drowned in the hurricane. After the train was swept from the rails, the Overseas Railroad was bankrupt. The pier project was abandoned, and the Overseas Highway replaced the railroad.

Considered part of the Oceanside Hurricane Monument, the plaque was paid for and erected by FDR's Works Progress Administration.

These structures are part of the Heritage Monument Trail established by the Matecumbe Historical Trust Corporation.

Address:
Bayside Channel 2 Piers
Mile Marker 73.1

....

Bayside Indian Wells

These wells were surrounded by an Indian Village 1,000 years ago.
—Plaque at the site

Ghost Story

The marker for the ancient Indian Wells is on the bay side in a wooded area of Islamorada near Island Christian Church. At night, the place swarms with mosquitos. One thousand years ago, Native Americans populated the Keys. It is thought they were driven there by attacks from other Native tribes.

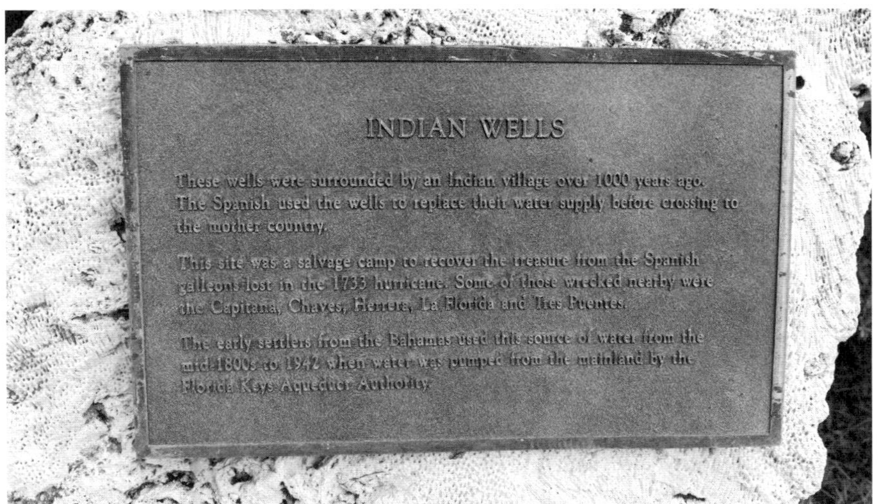

The Bayside Indian Wells marker.

The Native Americans found water and dug the wells. Water was also used in their ceremonies. It is known that the Calusas, and their ancestors, believed in supernatural beings and water spirits. They thought that when they died, their soul would be reincarnated in the body of a smaller animal and then a smaller animal—and so on until their soul was reunited with the earth. No one knows how long this takes. Is one thousand years long enough to shed the many skins of earthly life? It certainly makes one regard wildlife differently.

Behind the Indian Wells Historical Marker is a wooded area. The wells are sunk in bracken today and impossible to identify. Be respectful of any squirrels, deer, birds, even butterflies. They could represent the evolving spiritual destiny of a former Indian.

HISTORY

Fresh water was key for survival. There were only twenty-two spots for fresh water in the 125-mile chain of Keys. The wells at the Islamorada site could have been artesian wells, where water mounts to the surface because of force from an underground aquifer. Or they could have been depressions dug into the ground where water collected in the porous rock. Most of the ancient wells were fairly shallow. The tribes who created them were primarily fisherfolk.

The Native Americans were mostly driven from the Keys by disease, immigration, and the English slave trade. The few Natives remaining were absorbed into the Seminole tribes or worked as divers for the Spanish. The Spanish also used the site as a salvage camp, where they enjoyed the fresh water after a hard day of watching slaves recover treasure from wrecked ships.

Then came the Bahamians, who used the wells as their water source. The Bahamians were farmers who knew how to tend the rough, rocky soil so similar to that of their homeland. They grew their own food and survived.

It wasn't until 1942 that water was finally pumped to the Keys via a pipeline. The pipeline, built during World War II, follows the line of the Overseas Highway. It is problematic at times, and it is not unusual for visitors to the Keys to see huge water pipes lying on the side of the Overseas Highway while employees of the Florida Keys Aqueduct Authority retrench or make repairs. Sometimes the water main breaks and traffic is blocked on the islands along US 1, which forces businesses to close early. In 2023, the water main broke three times in one week.

It is also not unusual for locals to complain about Keys water pressure, especially during a shower on a hot day when the water is no more than a

The ancient site of the former Indian wells.

trickle. Sometimes when a resident puts quarters in a washing machine at a laundromat, there is not enough water to fill the basin.

We should all remember how the Indians, Spaniards, and Bahamians had to cope with water on the hard little Key they called home. Running water, however scanty, would have seemed like an unbelievable luxury.

Today the Indian Wells are a historic emblem of the Keys' eclectic history. The site and the historic marker are part of the Heritage Monument Trail established by the Matecumbe Historical Trust Corporation.

Address:
Islamorada
Mile Marker 83.8

....

CHEECA LODGE'S PIONEER CEMETERY

This lovely bud so young, so fair…
—*Excerpt from the inscription on Etta Pinder's grave*

Ghost Story

After the 1935 Labor Day hurricane, Upper Matecumbe was flattened: school, church, houses, stores, trees, post office. Some people say the only thing still standing was a white angel on the beach marking the grave of a fifteen-year-old girl, an only child named Etta Delores Pinder (the Pinders were one of the Keys' founding families). Some people say the statue was found on the highway, blown asunder by two-hundred-mile-per-hour winds. Regardless, it is one of few relics from the horrendous hurricane that was not completely destroyed. Holding a bouquet, the statue has one arm broken above the elbow and is missing inches of the top right wing. It survived the hurricane, though.

What's left today is a white picket fence and a few grave sites of the Parker, Pinder, and Russell families, homesteading pioneers whose descendants still live on the Rock. The tiny Pioneer Cemetery also holds at least fifty Bahamian settlers buried on Matecumbe Key.

This angel presides over the Pioneer Cemetery behind Cheeca Lodge.

It is not known if Etta haunts the Pioneer Cemetery, but someone certainly does after dark. People have felt the chilling presence of an otherworldly guest, and some visitors say they have felt a small hand take theirs.

History

The burial ground is unusual, located on the beach at the Cheeca Lodge & Spa. Visitors to the cemetery pass guests sunning on the beach, drinking, playing music from their speakers. It was entirely different around the turn of the twentieth century.

In 1910, a Methodist church was floated from its origin to an accessible grove of tropical trees that is now the Cheeca Lodge & Spa. The new setting for the church had been thoroughly routed, and the property belonged to the Matecumbe Methodist Church. A small school was built nearby. A cemetery was established near the church, in the custom of those days. It was known then and now as the Pioneer Cemetery.

Not only does the Cheeca Lodge keep the cemetery pristine, but it also allows nonpaying guests onto the complex to see it. One has to respect

Cheeca Lodge for its reverence of history. On the other hand, it's good advertising to let people walk the grounds. The Cheeca is way swanky. There are white sand beaches and tennis, pickleball, and volleyball courts. There are also yoga classes, snorkeling, water aerobics, and, of course, the spa. It has a fishing pier. And like at all Key resorts, the tiki bar is just one of many to pick from, along with its famous champagne brunch at Atlantic Edge on weekends.

Originally known as Casa Islamorado, it was the first hotel and restaurant on the island and part of the post–World War II boom. Then it was Islamorada Olney Inn, visited by President Harry Truman, who really loved the Keys and owned the "Little White House" in Key West. A fisherman's paradise, Islamorada quickly became known as the sport fishing capital of the world.

Destroyed by Hurricane Donna, Olney Inn was sold to Cynthia Twitchell, heiress of the A&P grocery chain fortune. She oversaw the building of the Cheeca Lodge—except for the golf course, which was created by Jack Nicklaus. Cynthia called the property Cheeca, uniting her nickname, Chee, and her husband's name, Carl, to create the lodge, a luxurious and fairly reasonably priced stay in the Upper Keys, even today. Famous movie stars, musicians, golf pros, and serious fishermen also frequented Cheeca. In fact, President George Bush Sr. established a bonefish tournament at the Cheeca Lodge that carried on for over a decade.

The Pioneer Cemetery at Cheeca Lodge in Islamorada is recognized as a site of historical importance by the Historical Association of Southern Florida. It is a valued piece of the Heritage Monument Trail established by the Matecumbe Historical Trust Corporation.

Address:
Cheeca Lodge & Spa
Mile Marker 81.7
81801 Overseas Highway
Islamorada, Florida
305 664 4651

. . . .

CHAPTER 3
MIDDLE KEYS

THE OLD SEVEN MILE BRIDGE

It is perfectly simple. All you have to do is build one concrete arch, and then another, and pretty soon you will find yourself in Key West.
—Henry Flagler

GHOST STORY

The internet features a story about a strange apparition haunting the old Seven Mile Bridge, a fisherman who uses human hands for bait. A more likely ghostly scenario involves the lives that were lost in the construction of the massive project. Rail and bridge builders succumbed to injuries from falls, crushing weights, even snake bites and crocodile attacks. Some contracted mosquito-borne illnesses such as yellow fever or dengue fever. Veterans died in a deadly hurricane.

Today, pedestrians who view the span of the seven-mile bridge from a grassy knoll near the old bridge may notice a plethora of green iguanas in the grass. The green iguana is one of three species prevalent on the islands and the most commonly seen. These reptiles take the sun out in the open, camouflaged by the grass. Iguanas have become invasive in the Keys, eating

Seven Mile Bridge, old and new.

Tailless iguana near the old Seven Mile Bridge.

plants and ruining landscaping. Perhaps someone captures them and dumps them near the bridge.

Iguanas were worshipped as holy by ancient civilizations, and the Mayans and the Aztecs believed iguanas were the reincarnated souls of dead warriors.

HISTORY

The railroad project began in 1909 and was completed in 1912. The origin of the rail was in Homestead, and the train went all the way to Key West. The Overseas Railroad connected all the islands.

The old bridge with the railroad trestles was the ambition of Henry Flagler of Standard Oil fame, one of the original visionaries of the railroad. Before the train, there was limited access to get to most of the islands except by boat or by ferry. On completion, the rails extended over one hundred miles on narrow trestles. However, no one anticipated the Labor Day hurricane of 1935, which changed so much about the destiny of the Keys, including methods of transportation accessing the elusive islands.

It began with good intentions. FDR offered hundreds of World War I vets employment in the Keys to work for the New Deal in his Works Progress Administration. There were bridges that needing building to replace ferries. Unfortunately, as part of the Civilian Conservation Corps, most of these brave vets lost their lives on that fateful Labor Day.

There were three camps of frame shacks, which the men built themselves, on Windley, Upper, and Lower Matecumbe Keys. As the hurricane approached on Labor Day, there was minimal staff, so the rescue train was delayed and ended up barreling right into the full force of the hurricane, which swept it off the tracks. Hundreds of people died, most of them veterans working for $1.50 a day.

Ernest Hemingway wrote an op-ed in *New Masses* magazine a few days later titled "Who Murdered the Vets?" He hurried to the Keys to join the rescue mission. He wrote eloquently of the squalor and devastation in the aftermath of the storm and of the multitude of bodies. "You could see them face up and face down in the mangroves," he wrote. There are monuments to the hurricane victims in Islamorada (see the preceding section "The Hurricane Memorials"). A congressional investigation ensued, and lawmakers determined that whoever was responsible was absolved. They deemed the hurricane and the loss of life an act of God.

After the rescue train and miles of rail were swept away by a tidal wave during the Labor Day hurricane, the Florida East Coast Railroad went bankrupt and was sold to the United States government. Thus, the Overseas Railroad eventually became the Overseas Highway—wider, with the old track as guardrails and the railroad bridges as the foundation. It ran west from Marathon to the Lower Keys. At one time, it was the longest bridge in the United States, and it is still the longest bridge in Florida. Its construction has been described as an engineering feat second only to building the Panama Canal.

The U.S. Navy moved in, and the road it erected over and along the old railroad was completed in 1938 and celebrated with fanfare. Automobiles were gaining popularity during the South Florida land boom, enabling "entrepreneurs" to sell swampland in Dade County. It made sense to them that the parcels of vacant land in the Upper, Middle, and Lower Keys should go up for sale as well. But there were scant ways to get prospective buyers onto the islands without railroad or road access. Moneyed men wanted to ensure that access to Key West continued. They succeeded. In 1939, Franklin Delano Roosevelt was driven over the seven-mile bridge on his way to Key West. The Overseas Highway had arrived.

The first bridge was narrow, and driving across the old rails at night with only the moonlight to guide you was a spooky experience. The modern bridge that exists today was completed in the 1980s. Two miles of the original bridge, from Marathon to Pigeon Key, are available for bike traffic and walkers. (The original seven-mile bridge continued south to Pigeon Key. The new bridge bypasses the tiny Key altogether.) The rest of the bridge is closed and dangerous to walk on because of its derelict infrastructure. A few trees grow right through the cracks in the concrete of the old bridge. Today, the two bridges run almost parallel across the same span of blue ocean.

The newer bridge closes for a couple of hours one day every April to host a seven-mile run commemorating the sacrifices and the efforts of men who built both the old and the new bridges. The original Seven Mile Bridge has also been featured in several movies, including *True Lies*, *License to Kill*, and *2 Fast 2 Furious.*

Both the old and new Seven Mile Bridges are engineering wonders, and it is picturesque on either span of concrete and steel, especially at sunrise or sunset, with spectacular seascapes of the Atlantic Ocean and the Gulf of Mexico (they meet around the location of the bridge). The sensation a driver experiences crossing the bridge is best explained by anonymous graffiti scratched on a beam of the old bridge: "These are the lost islands."

The old Seven Mile Bridge is listed on the National Register of Historic Places.

ADDRESS:
OLD SEVEN MILE BRIDGE
1240 OVERSEAS HIGHWAY
MARATHON, FLORIDA

....

CHAPTER 4
LOWER KEYS

OLD BAHIA HONDA BRIDGE

When the going gets weird, the weird turn pro.
—Hunter S. Thompson

GHOST STORY

In March, April, and May, it is not unusual for fishermen to see half a dozen bull or hammerhead sharks under the old Bahia Honda bridge, also known as the Ghost Bridge of the Florida Keys. They attack tarpon in the way lions attack gazelles. This is nothing new. In prehistoric times, Calusa Indians would have come upon the megalodon shark, which once swam in these waters—and makes the great white shark look like Charlie the Tuna.

Not to be outdone, for decades, local anglers beguiled tourists with stories of a giant hammerhead shark named Big Mo. (Mo stands for "monster.") The eighteen-foot hammerhead with eyeballs "as big as baseballs" supposedly weighs half a literal ton. And most stories put Big Mo under the old Bahia Honda Bridge.

Bridges, unfortunately, are vantage points for future floaters. If someone fell, was pushed, or actually jumped off the highest point of the Bahia Honda bridge, one can almost anticipate the sight of the feeding frenzy that would occur in the water and the screams of the victim as she succumbed to the shark attack.

Tourists visiting the bridge at sunset have reported a shadowy figure lurking among the girders. Beachgoers rushed to the edge of the shore, shading their eyes, to determine where the splashing and screaming was coming from. There was no answer.

Big Mo restrained himself or was off under another bridge that day in 1979 when "Bahia Honda Keys Jane Doe," a teenager, was found under the south side of the Bahia Honda Bridge. Authorities suspect she jumped and drowned, as no obvious injuries were found. Locals speculated she could have

The old Bahia Honda bridge.

been a Cuban refugee whose flimsy boat of refuge sank. Although her body was untouched by the giant hammerhead and her likeness reconstructed by forensics, Bahia Honda Keys Jane Doe was never identified, and the mystery of her death was never solved. If there is a ghost connected to the old bridge, it is surely this young girl, forever sixteen, wistful and unwilling to be consigned to history unnamed. But at least Big Mo spared her the indignity of anonymity and never being named at all.

History

The name Bahia Honda is Spanish for "deep bay." A little south of Marathon lies the Bahia Honda State Park, which has a water depth of thirty-five feet and one of the few good beaches in the Florida Keys.

Calusa Beach comes complete with a view of the derelict, skeletal, rusting old Bahia Honda bridge. The old two-lane crossing is cracked, and parts are falling into the ocean. It's been closed for over forty years.

When the Overseas Highway opened to automobiles in 1938, the old Bahia Honda train bridge's construction was noticeably altered. The road traveled over the top of the old train bridge, sixty-five feet above the deep waters and the strong currents. It was an engineering challenge, to say the least. Built on girders, it was a very narrow bridge, and you were way up in the air. Passengers were warned to keep their heads and arms inside the car. Truckers took in their side mirrors. The highway was built atop the trusses because the bridge's width didn't allow for two lanes of traffic.

In 1972, Monroe County Mayor Harry Harris cut the ribbon for the new four-lane Bahia Honda bridge, which was operational by 1980. The old bridge is listed on the National Register of Historic Places.

Address:
Bahia Honda State Park
36850 Overseas Highway, Big Pine Key

....

NO NAME PUB AND NO NAME KEY

A nice place if you can find it.
—Old Keys saying

Ghost Story

For many years, the electrical and the telephone lines ended right after the No Name Pub. That was where the oldest bar in the Keys, founded in 1936, began its legend.

Originally, the No Name Pub was a bait and tackle general store with "storage"—i.e., a brothel—upstairs. Because of the remote nature of the pub and the general lawlessness that governed the early Keys, it is said that when a prostitute became pregnant by one of the rough men who frequented the upper floor, she kept it to herself. Otherwise, both she and her infant's lives were in danger. Customers didn't want the entanglements of an illegitimate child or its wanton mother. Sometimes, the woman wouldn't go quietly. It was said that the vast wilderness and scrub behind the old building held gruesome secrets that would not bear the light of day.

Then there is the ghost of the No Name Hermit, whose real name was Nicholas Matcovich. In 1870, he lived in Key West for a time with his Bahamian wife, but he was a true introvert who preferred the sparsely populated No Name Key. He built a shack there, which his wife endured for a few years before moving back to Key West. Matcovich eventually homesteaded his land and grew many species of fruit trees, attracting the attention of William Krome, who became a kind of mentor. Legend has it that Matcovich was loath to leave the Keys even in death and sightings of his lingering specter persist to this day.

More recent ghosts may remain as well. In 1988, law enforcement deputies found a naked body on a deserted road on No Name Key. Her jaw

The No Name Pub on No Name Key, a ferry stop before the Overseas Highway was built.

was broken, she had been stabbed and mutilated, had abrasions on her body and a rope around her neck. All indications were that she had been dragged by a car. Her heart was missing.

The victim's name was Lisa Sanders, a nursing student, and before the twenty-year-old died, she attended a party on a remote area of the sparsely populated Key. She left alone to walk back to her trailer in the early evening. Some amateur sleuths speculate that her killer could have been serial killer Charlie Brandt, who lived on Big Pine Key and was allegedly present at the party. Regardless, the case is still listed as unsolved.

As a postscript, Brandt is known for the gruesome murders of his wife and niece during a hurricane retreat at a home in Maitland, Florida, near Orlando, in 1989. His niece's body was also mutilated and her heart removed. Brandt hanged himself in the garage.

History

Visitors dwindled with the opening of the Overseas Highway in 1938. Once bridges replaced ferries, No Name Pub's location became decidedly obscure. People went to great lengths to find it.

No Name Pub is located on Big Pine Key, a National Key Deer Refuge and Nature Trail. Plentiful fresh water attracts the Key deer, the iguanas, and possibly the chickens that also comprise No Name Key's wildlife.

Perhaps in ancient times as the waters rose, the deer were isolated on Big Pine and No Name Key. Key deer are about the size of a large dog and are found only in these piney surroundings. They used to be hunted by Native Americans and their hides used for clothing. Poaching and traffic in the twentieth century further decimated their numbers. Key deer are an endangered species, and it is a federal offense to kill one.

People sometimes come to the Keys to avoid just that sort of scrutiny. At the No Name Pub, the upstairs brothel was no more, but the Keys were still kind of lawless in the '60s, '70s, and '80s when it came to drugs. Pot and cocaine were easily accessible. People who trafficked in illegal contraband or who helped themselves to the "square groupers" that washed up on the shore often disappeared. Either the police took the scavengers to jail or smugglers chucked them into the intercoastal. Still, there was a lot of cash from drugs and limited ways to spend it on the Rock. At the No Name Pub, patrons started hanging dollar bills on the walls, beams, and ceilings.

Dollar bills stapled to the ceilings and walls at the No Name Pub.

It is estimated there are $900,000 worth of $1 bills at the No Name Pub from people all over the world. A couple hundred dollars a day go up from tourists. Most of the bills are signed with a marker the waitress provides. Some bills have riddles or short anecdotes written on them.

The pub used to have a pool table in less animated times, but it disappeared to accommodate more tables to seat tourists. If you want a memorable lunch at a Keys icon, turn right off US 1 onto Key Deer and Watson Boulevards to find the No Name Pub. The menu is mostly bar food, pizza, conch fritters, chowder, and burgers. Don't forget to staple a dollar to the wall with your name on it. It's good luck.

ADDRESS:
NO NAME PUB
30813 WATSON BOULEVARD, BIG PINE KEY
305 872 9115

. . . .

CHAPTER 5
KEY WEST

THE BELLMAN AT THE CASA MARINA RESORT

I knew that this job would be too much for me.
—President Warren G. Harding

GHOST STORY

The one-hundred-plus-year-old resort generates no reviews from guests claiming that lights go on and off, that televisions are arbitrarily muted and unmuted, or that there is the scent of free-floating cigar smoke or perfume in the halls and rooms. There are no reports of whistling or voices on the stairs when no one else is there. The ghosts of the Vanderbilts or even Henry Flagler are not at large.

If there are haunted guest rooms in the Casa Marina, the occupants are keeping it to themselves. It is not on the list of haunted hotels in Key West. The upper floors are mostly occupied by staff, who have not reported any hauntings. The somber shadows of the resort's famous guests are not in evidence.

The ghost story has to do with the iconic bronze statue of a bellman lighting a cigarette near the main entrance of the resort. The life-size statue was constructed by John Seward Johnson, grandson of Robert Johnson, the

The smoking bellman at the Casa Marina.

cofounder of the Johnson & Johnson corporation. The statue was created from a cast of a real person, whose spirit seems to have lingered.

Guests often use the bellman replica for photo ops and decorate the slouching statue with tiaras and ball caps. Some of them report a slight shock when they touch the statue, although bronze is a mediocre conductor of electricity. Others claim his stance has shifted to the right over the years. And one memorable anecdote concerns a guest stepping out of the lobby at midnight and seeing a bright flare of flame and a thin trail of smoke emanating from the motionless statue.

HISTORY OF THE RESORT

The Casa Marina is Henry Flagler's last luxury hotel, erected for the same purpose as the Hotel Ponce de Leon in St. Augustine. The oil man and developer wanted a swanky destination to house his rich and famous guests. Flagler sought a Spanish Colonial look for the resort, and Thomas Hastings and John M. Carrere (architects of New York's Metropolitan Opera House, the New York Public Library, and official buildings in Washington, D.C.) honored his wishes. The Casa Marina, known as the House by the Sea, was the last stop on the Florida East Coast Overseas Railway.

Construction began in 1912, but Flagler died from a fall at his Palm Beach home the following year and never saw the grand opening in 1920. President Warren Harding celebrated in his stead, followed by a slew of prominent folks, including Rudy Vallee, Susan Hayworth, Robert Frost, Wallace Stevens, Gregory Peck, and other celebrities and dignitaries.

The resort was commandeered twice by military events. During World War II, it was owned by the navy for a few years to house officers. In 1962, during the Bay of Pigs Cuban missile crisis, the resort was filled with military personnel and surrounded by barbed wire. In the '60s, the Westinghouse Corporation rented it for a few years to train Peace Corps volunteers.

Empty from 1967 to 1976, in the '80s, it leased out rooms as apartments for anywhere from $300 to $1,300 a month. It was purchased by a variety of owners at different times, including the Waldorf Astoria. Today, owned by Hilton as part of its Curio Collection, it is one of an international pool of eclectic hotels. Only a ten-minute walk from the historic district, the Casa Marina July Fourth fireworks draw spectators from all over the island.

The resort is worth over $65 million, and the land it occupies is valued at twice that. The exterior walls are twenty-two inches of poured concrete from the same material used for the pylons on the old Overseas Railroad. The Casa Marina boasts eleven thousand square feet of space, 311 rooms, two swimming pools, suites, and a private beach. A 750,000-gallon concrete cistern installed in the 1920s is still operational, but in recent years, the Casa Marina has undergone a $79 million renovation of its rooms, landscaping, furniture, activity piers, and amenities.

Walking into the lobby with its Dade County pine wooden floors, high ceilings patterned with black-and-silver cypress, pillars, round-top floor-to-ceiling windows, and natural sunlight is a rare chance to experience the nostalgia of the 1920s. And outside the front door is a bronze bellman who doesn't like to be interrupted from his cigarette break.

The Casa Marina Key West is on the National Register of Historic Places.

Address:
Casa Marina Key West
1500 Reynolds Street, Key West
305 296 3535

. . . .

LA CONCHA KEY WEST

Never travel with anyone you don't love.
—Ernest Hemingway

Ghost Story

Built in 1926 by Carl Aubuchon, La Concha Key West could also go by the name Thirteen Ghosts. The imposing luxury hotel, the tallest building in Key West, was the scene of thirteen suicides in the twentieth and twenty-first centuries. All these self-destructive people plunged from the roof to their death. One was a woman dumped (not literally) by her boyfriend. Another was a lawyer who tried to make his suicide look like murder for insurance reasons. One man downed a drink for courage before he jumped, and so on. It's almost as if they were all possessed.

The fifth floor is considered the most haunted in the hotel because of the death of an employee (either a waiter or a busboy, depending on who's telling the story) who backed into an empty elevator shaft. Ever since, guests and staff report hearing his ghostly voice calling for help from the bowels of the elevator.

Guests of La Concha report all the usual paranormal activity of haunted hotels: cold spots, lights turning on and off, strange shadows when no one is there, missing or moved items. One couple on their honeymoon reported late-night spirit shenanigans, such as the faucet repeatedly turning on and off and the toilet flushing and flushing. No one was in the bathroom.

Supposedly, the thirteen suicides congregate as ghosts on the roof. Guests report having drinks snatched out of their hands, particularly wine. Don't make a fuss; at La Concha it is wise to share your spirits with the spirits.

HISTORY

The hotel rose in 1926 and took up half a city block on Duval Street. The 160-room, reinforced concrete, steel-girded La Concha Key West was built in the Spanish Colonial Revival style, featuring carved doors, curved columns, and a tiled roof. Boasting private baths, a rooftop bar, an electric elevator, and a swimming pool, La Concha was the go-to destination for the rich and famous, including Ernest Hemingway, Tennessee Williams, and President Harry Truman.

Known as the Key West Colonial during the Great Depression of the 1930s, the hotel fell into disrepair exacerbated by the devasting hurricane of 1935, which destroyed the East Coast Overseas Railroad. It wasn't until the Overseas Highway was built that business started picking up, but the hotel continued to deteriorate. Finally, the hotel was fully renovated in the 1980s.

That was almost fifty years ago. In the ensuing years, its original name, La Concha, was restored, and the hotel again underwent extensive renovation,

The fully renovated La Concha Hotel.

which was completed in 2025. The renovation included Cuban-style décor, new furniture, a rooftop swimming pool, a coffee bar, a restaurant, and more. Located in the heart of Old Town, the hotel is a short jaunt away from the sunset revelries in Mallory Square.

La Concha Key West is on the National Register of Historic Places.

Address:
La Concha Key West
430 Duval Street, Key West
305 296 2991

....

FOGARTY'S AND THE FLYING MONKEYS SALOON

I love living my life in flip-flops. I met a guy in the islands a while ago who told me he hadn't worn a pair of shoes in three years! I thought, "Man, that's the life!"
—Kenny Chesney

Ghost Story

Apparently, owner Joe Walsh of Fogarty's Restaurant and Flying Monkeys Saloon is not afraid of ghosts. However, he took no chances.

There is a ghost that haunts the 125-plus-year-old building. It was the private home of a Key West mayor, a restaurant, in later years an inn, and then a Hooter's restaurant. Customers reported a presence and some strange activity with shoes.

There is no documented evidence of ghost sightings when the establishment was Fogarty's restaurant. But when it was an inn, guests complained of someone waking them up at night by touching their feet. When it was a Hooter's restaurant, there were some rooms on the third floor for waitresses. In the morning, when the women woke up, they found their shoes rearranged on one side of the room. Sometimes, during a shift, their shoelaces would untie three or four times a night.

Fogarty's and the Flying Monkeys Saloon.

Walsh believed the ghost would settle down if his establishment retained its original owner's name. From all accounts, it's a step in the right direction.

HISTORY

The first home on the site burned down, but it was rebuilt in 1887 by Charles Curry, son of a millionaire. After he died, a Dr. Joseph Fogarty married Curry's daughter and either bought the house or received it as a wedding present in 1900.

By all accounts, Fogarty was an ambitious and energetic man. He ran for mayor and served for six terms. He was pressed during the era of Prohibition to take steps to turn Key West dry. He declined, perhaps because of his love of entertaining.

As the host of lavish parties celebrating politicians and developers, he feted Henry Flagler, Grover Cleveland, and William Taft in the Victorian house on Duval Street. In fact, he and his wife were there to greet Flagler in 1912 when the Standard Oil magnate and luxury hotelier stepped off the Overseas Railroad to Key West for the first and the last time of his life.

After the Fogartys died, the house stood empty until the 1970s, when it was re-created into a succession of businesses. The present-day Fogarty's has been around for decades. The name Flying Monkey at Fogarty's refers to the bar where the line of frozen Florida-themed drink machines churns out variations of rumrunners for tourists. The bar features painted murals by Captain Outrageous, a famous white-bearded Key West artist who died in 2001.

Walsh restored the name of the property to Fogarty's. The place is a tremendously popular spot for an outdoor meal and its famous frozen drinks, which are often carried into the street in plastic to-go cups. According to the Key West municipal code, open containers of alcoholic beverages are forbidden in public areas. However, local law enforcement ignores it unless someone is causing a ruckus. In fact, there aren't a lot of rules in Key West, although there are laws.

Joe Walsh found this out the hard way on the most profitable night for Duval businesses other than Fantasy Fest. Walsh got in trouble on New Year's Eve 2021 when he refused to close the bar two hours before midnight in keeping with the city's lingering COVID-19 curfew. Customers protested, and six people were arrested, including Walsh. They all spent the New Year in jail. "Is Key West now going to be a place that someone is trying to make not fun?" Walsh asked.

Hardly. Fogarty's and the Flying Monkeys Saloon host the city's legendary Red Party every Fantasy Fest to raise money for public schools and scholarships. Everyone dresses in red, the decorations are red, the lights are red, and so on. It's a bash on par with Dr. Joe's famed extravaganzas.

The Fogarty Mansion is a historic site and the recipient of a Key West Historic Marker.

ADDRESS:
FOGARTY'S AND THE FLYING MONKEYS SALOON
225 DUVAL STREET, KEY WEST
305 294 7525

....

THE ARTIST HOUSE AND ROBERT THE DOLL

Robert did it.
—Robert Gene Otto

GHOST STORY

The Artist House is a luxury inn named in honor of its former occupant Robert Gene Otto, a well-known painter and Key West native. It is also the former home of Robert the Doll, a 117-plus-year-old artifact famous throughout Key West and the world. How Gene acquired the doll is a matter of debate. Some say that when the artist was a boy, a servant of Caribbean descent gave him the doll. Another tale has Gene's grandfather giving him the doll after a trip to Germany. According to the most likely account, Gene's grandfather gave him the doll, and the servant gave the doll its powers.

Regardless of the origin of the unusual gift, Gene named the doll Robert. Robert is made of cloth and stuffed with straw, measures forty inches tall, and is dressed in a sailor suit that likely belonged to Gene. His fabric face is weathered, and he has beady eyes. He carries a mangy stuffed dog.

Gene and Robert were inseparable. However, Gene's parents noticed that their son blamed the doll for his own transgressions, saying, "Robert did it." At least that's what they thought—until the time there was a terrible ruckus in Gene's room with the bed overturned, toys everywhere, and their son in a corner, screaming. They took Robert the Doll away.

Robert the Doll with his companion dog.

Years later, after studying and working abroad, Gene came home to the Artist House in Key West with his wife, Ann. Gene rescued his old friend Robert the Doll and brought him back to his home in the attic, where Ann insisted he stay. Instead, over time, neighbors reported seeing Robert the Doll in almost every window of the stately Artist House.

Today, Robert the Doll resides in the Fort East Martello Museum. Ghost tour guides insist that Robert was the inspiration for the frightful

The Artist House during Fantasy Fest.

The Artist House on Eaton Street.

Chucky films. There's also a lot of documented evidence that visitors to the East Martello Museum suffer bad luck if they mock Robert or even take his picture without permission. The only solution to end Robert's curse is to write him a letter of apology, which a museum employee reads aloud to him. There is a streaming loop of these letters on video near the doll's display.

HISTORY

Between the history of its former resident Robert the Doll and the lore of Eaton Street as one of the most haunted streets in the United States, you might say the odds of a supernatural event at the Artist House are high.

However, its website does not affirm that assumption, stating instead that not one guest has reported anything unusual during their stay.

Built in the 1890s, this wooden Colonial Queen Anne–style bed-and-breakfast has seven rooms individually decorated in the Victorian style. In the character of the period, the house is adorned with a turret, bay windows, and a veranda. Guests must rely on public parking, although it is within easy walking distance of Old Town. According to local lore, you may encounter Hemingway's ghost along the way. Let the Artist House know.

The Artist House is on the National Directory of Haunted Places.

Address:
The Artist House
534 Eaton Street, Key West
305 296 3977

....

HEMINGWAY HOME AND MUSEUM

A damned haunted house.
—Pauline Hemingway

Ghost Story

There have been sightings of Ernest and Pauline Hemingway in the high-walled Whitehead Street location where they both lived for eight years. The tapping of typewriter keys is sometimes heard from the upper level of the old carriage house separated by a bridge from the upstairs bedroom. And why not? Ernest had a good time in Key West despite his marriage to Pauline crumbling. He wrote in the morning and went to Sloppy Joe's, the old one on Greene Street, in the afternoon. Once he dragged back a urinal. During an afternoon of drinking, he met his third future ex-wife, the journalist Martha Gellhorn. He ditched Pauline, covered the Spanish Civil War with Martha, and then moved to Cuba. But he could be back.

Further evidence of Ernest's lingering ethereal presence in the Hemingway home is his cats. Since the 1930s, polydactyl (six-toed) cats have roamed the

Above: The Hemingway house conducts daily tours.

Left: Six-toed Hemingway cats roam the old house and gardens today.

premises. Sixty Hemingway cats live in the old house and gardens today. They even have their own cemetery. They are descended from Snow White, a six-toed cat Ernest received from a ship captain. The digitally unchallenged cats are supposed to bring good luck. In that case, the Hemingway ghosts and their incompatible relationship should stay away.

It is likely, however, that Pauline is the presence that haunts the house. She stayed in Key West when Ernest left her, and she made many friends and community connections during those years. She even reunited with Hattie, Ernest's first wife, on at least one memorable visit covered by the local news.

However, her death was particularly unpleasant. Visiting her sister in California, she passed away from a brain aneurysm after arguing on the phone with Ernest about their son Gregory, who went by the name Gloria. Gloria was arrested for cross-dressing and using a woman's bathroom. Pauline died.

Pauline is buried in Hollywood. Nevertheless, since she passed, there have been reports of her shadow standing by the Key West Garden gate or at the top of the stairs. Pauline was a chain-smoker, and at times there is a whiff of her cigarette smoke in the air.

History

Pauline Pfeiffer was a society gal who came from old money family. One of her relatives bought the house on Whitehead Street for the newlyweds not too long after she married Ernest.

Previously owned by a wrecker, the French Colonial house was built by Asa Tift in 1895. Both the Hemingways lived there from 1931 to 1939, and the house needed considerable restoration, which was mostly handled by Pauline. The humid climate loosened the plaster; there were repairs on the sloping roof. A limestone privacy wall was erected.

Pauline put in an expensive saltwater swimming pool, which she paid for herself. Hemingway had a tantrum anyway and threw a penny into the wet cement beside the pool, claiming the contractor had taken his last cent. That was baloney. Hemingway was so careless with money that after his death, his widow found uncashed royalty checks in boxes he'd stashed at Sloppy Joes.

A former *Vogue* journalist sent on assignments to Paris, Pauline gave it up to live on an island and devote herself to home, children, and a husband who sustained his most prolific literary output during their time together. He also drank too much and cheated on her, but Pauline did what she could

Above: The wall encasing the Hemingway house that Asa Tift built.

Left: Hemingway's office, where he wrote *A Farewell to Arms*.

Opposite: Hemingway's saltwater pool.

to hang on. It was futile. Her husband and the woman he met at Sloppy Joe's fled to a literal war zone, which seemed to characterize Hemingway's preferred ambiance when it came to marriage as well. In 1940, Hemingway married Martha Gellhorn, ensuring the launch of yet another disastrous relationship.

Pauline did not remarry. She lived in the house until her death in 1951. The house stood vacant for years until the sons auctioned it off. It opened as a museum in 1964, a few years after Ernest's suicide. There was a minor scandal in the '70s when someone made off with a Picasso-designed clock in the shape of a cat, but the item was recovered. A facsimile was displayed in its place from then on.

Visitors can view Hemingway's old manual typewriter and writing desk; he often wrote standing up. There are first editions of his books, photographs, letters—even his moth-eaten hunting trophies. For those wanting to channel the Hemingway spirit, a purchase of $1,500 nets an evening of the "Hemingway Home Evening Writing Experience," where, for three hours, a lucky visitor is granted access to the home, the grounds, and, of course, the Hemingway cats.

The house is a National Historic Landmark and appears on the National Directory of Haunted Places.

Address:
Hemingway Home and Museum
907 Whitehead Street, Key West
305 294 1136

....

AUDUBON HOUSE AND TROPICAL GARDENS

I have a rival in every bird.
—Lucy Audubon

Ghost Story

Paranormal societies certify that the Audubon House is haunted, although I am unsure how much activity a ghost must arouse to obtain such a license. Using EVP (electronic voice phenomena) detectors, ghost hunters have heard laughter on the third floor, which sounds routine for an EVP. It is rumored there are graves of people buried in the garden under the brick passageways. But no one has used a buried body detector to public knowledge.

Certainly, the ghost is not John James Audubon, who never set foot in the house. The house wasn't even located on Whitehead and Green when Audubon was in Key West. The artist was fond of the Keys, particularly the Dry Tortugas, famous for its rookery. Audubon killed thousands of the birds he drew for the revered elephant folios containing his *Birds of America*. He was obsessed with birds, which contributed to the bitterness of his wife, Lucy, who was practically the sole breadwinner throughout their marriage while Audubon hunted, shot, and posed his prey. But it is not John, Lucy, or the birds who haunt the Audubon house. They have no history here despite the name, which was bestowed for Audubon's contributions to ornithology and not his excesses.

The Audubon House in Key West once hosted the famous elephant folios.

A view of the lush garden at the Audubon House in Key West.

If there is haunting, it is more likely done by Captain John Geiger, whose family and descendants lived in the house for over one hundred years. A middle-aged woman wearing a long blue dress has been sighted multiple times and identified as Lucretia, Geiger's mother.

Captain Geiger was a Conch (Key West native), a wrecker, and ironically, a member of a crew who chased pirates away, perhaps in the Mosquito Fleet, an anti-piracy squad. As a harbor pilot, he salvaged booty from the wrecks. He was very rich when he built the pine house now located on Whitehead. Clearly, he never wanted to leave.

Guests and docents see Geiger at the foot of the stairs, walking the grounds, looking out one of the windows. There are rumors of buried treasure; Geiger was a sea captain, after all. If you know anything about ghosts, you know they like to hang around buried swag.

HISTORY

There is a possibility that the two-story house was moved to this particular location for a reason. Whitehead and Greene Streets have a lot of pedestrian traffic, and the wood-frame American Classic Revival–style home was a testament to Geiger's wealth, which he didn't mind people knowing about. But by the end of the 1950s, such appreciation for architecture was not in evidence as historic homes and buildings were torn down in record numbers in favor of modern structures.

The Geiger House was slated to make way for a gas station. Mitchell Wolfson bought it instead and restored it, setting an example for the whole city. In 1960, the Geiger property became the Audubon House Museum, a movement dedicated to conservation, despite Audubon's killing sprees with endangered birds. Some of the house's antiques date to the nineteenth century, and in the 1980s, two volumes of Audubon's original elephant folios were available for public viewing. Someone stole them, they were found, and today the folios are under lock and key in a museum in Miami, although the Big Orange is hardly an incorruptible haven from random crime.

Touring the Audubon house today, the viewer observes antiques dating to the nineteenth century, some artwork, and, of course, the gardens. The acre of ground containing the Audubon Museum in Key West includes a butterfly garden, a nineteenth-century cookhouse (kitchens were separate from houses in those days), an orchid garden, and many native and nonnative flowers, trees, and plants. Included is the Geiger tree, which Audubon named after the famous wrecker. (One of the Key Islands was named after Geiger as well.) On a smaller scale, the Audubon gardens are similar to the famous Leu Gardens in Orlando, renowned for the beauty and diversity of its blooms.

The Audubon House is listed on the National Register of Historic Places and on the National Directory of Haunted Places.

Address:
The Audubon House
205 Whitehead Street, Key West
305 294 2116

....

TRUMAN'S LITTLE WHITE HOUSE

I've a notion to move the capital to Key West and just stay.
—Harry Truman

Ghost Story

There are sightings of the ghost of former U.S. President Harry Truman at his birthplace home in Missouri but scarcely any at the Little White House in Key West, Florida's only presidential site. However, there is no doubt Truman loved Key West. He visited the southernmost city eleven times for a total of 175 days, more than any other president before or since. There is a picture of him sitting in a convertible looking relaxed and wearing an aloha shirt and a safari hat.

Constructed in 1890, the Truman Annex where the Little White House is contained was intended for lodging naval officers. After the Truman administration, there were inexplicable dark shadows around the converted naval barracks, plaguing maintenance workers. In the 1980s, an editor and two reporters from the *Key West Citizen* spent the night there—stayed in Harry Truman's room, as a matter of fact. The newspaper carried their reports of seeing two ghosts, a man and a woman.

Thomas Edison stayed there for six months, designing weapons for the navy to use in World War I. Alan Brown in his book *Ghosts of the Gulf Coast*

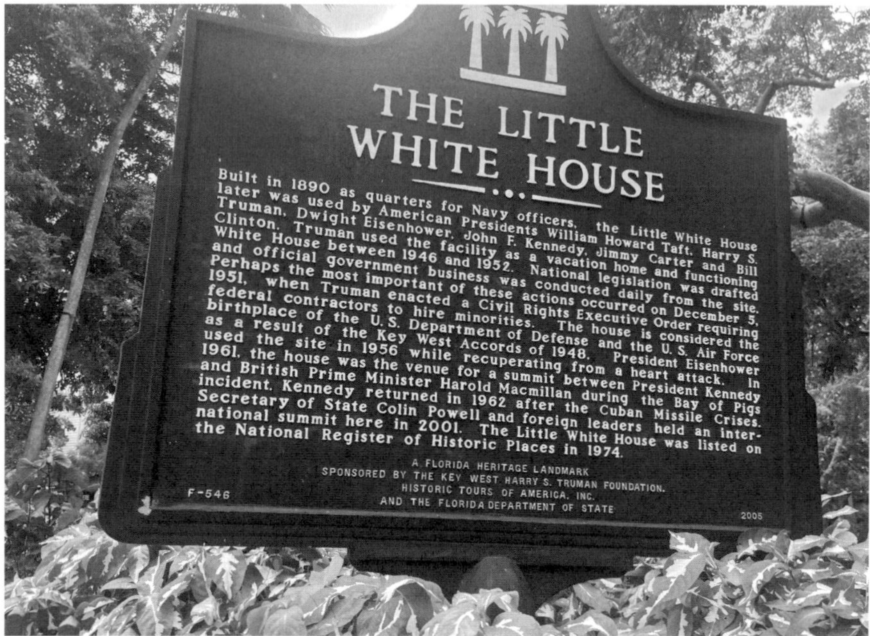

President Truman came to Key West eleven times during his term in office.

describes an incident with President Truman and two of his aides in the parlor of the Little White House. Truman was playing Edison's recording of "Mary Had a Little Lamb" when the front door opened inexplicably. There were footsteps, the sound of the phonograph lid crashing shut, and then the noisy exit of an unseen spirit.

History

The gated Truman Annex in Old Town is only a few minutes' walking distance from Mallory Square. It is mostly painted white, shuttered, and in good repair. That was not always true. According to the U.S. Department of the Navy, in the 1980s, the nineteenth-century buildings were a mess:

> *All facilities* [at the Truman Annex] *were suffering from considerable damage due to neglect, weather, and vandalism. Copper flashing had been removed from the roofs. Interior wiring, copper piping, plumbing fixtures, and lighting fixtures had been removed from the buildings, leaving severely damaged walls and ceilings. In most buildings, windows were left open to*

the weather, causing significant water damage to interiors. Most buildings had been broken into and had material stolen or vandalized.

In 1987, ownership of the Little White House was transferred to Key West. The city cleaned it up and established a museum. Presidents are still free to stay there, although tours would stop if that occurred.

President Taft was the first president to visit the wooden Key West house with its wraparound porches and shuttered blinds. President Clinton was the last. Important world events were decided at the president's abode in Key West. In 1948, President Truman initiated the creation of the Department of Defense from the Little White House in what was known as the Key West Agreement. President Kennedy negotiated strategy from the house in Key West during the Bay of Pigs nuclear crisis.

The museum is filled with furniture and mementos from the Truman era, including his famous poker table. Tripadvisor lists the Little White House as one of the top ten U.S. tours. Truman's Little White House is listed on the National Register of Historic Places and on the National Directory of Haunted Places.

Address:
Truman's Little White House
111 Front Street, Naval Air Station, Key West
305 294 9911

....

FORT EAST MARTELLO TOWER MUSEUM

Even when I'm done with something,
they think it's just garbage because it's made out of junk.
—Stanley Papio

Ghost Story

This place is really haunted. By a lot of ghosts. It's rated the tenth most haunted place in America by Ghost Key West haunted tours.

First, this has been Robert the Doll's home since he was removed from the Artist House. Employees of the museum claim that items fly off shelves and the lights go on and off when Robert is riled. They read letters of apology to the demonic doll from visitors who've crossed him and suffered the consequences. Robert wants respect, and viewers would do well to greet him and ask his permission before taking a picture. Otherwise, expect scalding beverages to spill, tires to go flat, fresh camera batteries to die. Seriously.

According to David Nolan's Haunted Key West website, there are other haunted artifacts in the museum such as Civil War relics and accompanying spirits. A Cuban trio, who perished at sea, reportedly hangs around the homemade raft that brought them in form, if not substance, to the Florida shore.

A cigar maker eternally rolls tobacco leaves at his old workbench. There is a ghost cat who used up all his lives. The museum was once a hospital, and psychics claim the souls of dead soldiers are rife throughout the building. There is a hearse from the notorious funeral home that once hosted a corpse who paralleled Faulkner's famous short story "A Rose for Emily" (see the section "Dean Lopez Horse-Drawn Hearse"). The headstone of the unfortunate Elena Milagro de Hoyos is rumored to be in the fort as well.

Entrance to the Fort East Martello Tower Museum.

Letters of apology scroll on the screen behind Robert the Doll at the East Martello Museum.

A unique and unforgettable display of folk-art sculptures constructed by the late welder and artist "Barefoot" Stanley Papio occupies the grounds and tower, with titles such as *Courthouse Scene*, *Bowlegged Bride*, *Sit and Think*, and *Rabbit*. One could wander around for hours accumulating trivia and determining whether the pasties on the *Las Vegas Model* sculpture are beer or soda caps.

The Key West Art and Historical Society hosted a Papio Kinetic Sculpture Parade for a few years on Duval Street, featuring a movable artistic feast of sculptures. According to a local blog, *The Blue Paper*, the society "encouraged the community to invoke the spirit of Papio by putting together their own kinetic sculpture float teams or art bike." Floats titled Peace Train and Where the Wild Things Are were the result.

Papio ghost vibes are everywhere.

HISTORY

Fort East Martello Tower is a defensive fort, similar to fifteenth-century Mediterranean structures. It has a square shape, identical to its sister fort at West Martello Tower. Fort East Martello sits in the shadow of Key West International, amid a few benches and roosting chickens. The roar of jet craft is loud. The roar of the present does not, however, drown out the history of the past. Thousands of tourists visit the former Union stronghold every year.

Although it played no part in its battles, construction of the fort started during the Civil War, when the War Department issued a call for two towers on either end of the island. Think back 150 years and imagine trying to obtain and pay for shipments of bricks coming from Pensacola to the Deep South during a war. When the bricks arrived, the soon-to-be freed slaves

Fort East Martello Tower Museum folk art exhibit.

were not enthusiastic about commencing backbreaking labor under the sun for no pay. Yellow fever outbreaks also delayed the completion of both the East and West Martello Towers. In fact, the forts were never completed, which is typical of most fort construction in Florida.

The fort moldered, left behind by the army, until the 1950s, when the Key West Art and Historical Society took on the task of restoring the building and converting it into a museum. At the time, it didn't even have a roof. Today it is an important testament to Key West history and its art.

The building is a National Historic Landmark. *USA Today* included the fort in its list of "Ten Most Haunted Destinations."

ADDRESS:
FORT EAST MARTELLO TOWER MUSEUM
3501 S. ROOSEVELT BOULEVARD, KEY WEST
305 296 3913

....

WEST MARTELLO TOWER MUSEUM

Are you sure about this location?
—Army Corps of Engineers

Ghost Story

In 1861, construction began on the East and West Martello Towers in Key West. There was some discussion over the location of the west tower, which fronted a beach that was, literally, a huge graveyard. The U.S. Army Corps of Engineers pointed to a map they'd made of the spot where African refugees were rescued from a slave ship. Hundreds of the kidnapped people consequently expired and were buried on the spot. A local engineer asked the bureaucrats in Washington, D.C., "Are you sure about this location?"

Someone in D.C. said, "Start building."

There are mixed reports about bodies buried under the West Martello Tower. The Mel Fisher Maritime Heritage Society did an archaeological survey, which found no human remains there. Yet according to an article by Emily Whalton written in 1987 for the *Key West Citizen*, human remains were found when the foundation was dug in 1861. Apparently, the site originally boarded a pesthouse, where people dying of communicable diseases were sent to perish. And in the front and back of the proposed site for the west tower were the unmarked beach graves of kidnapped West Africans from an illegal slave ship apprehended in the coastal waters by the U.S. Navy. Some of the bodies are buried across the street from the site. The West Tower stood, and stands today, in the middle of the Higgs Beach unmarked graveyard.

Construction on the tower continued throughout the Civil War. It was never completed, and after the war, it fell into disrepair. Townspeople took its bricks for their own purposes. Many years later, a couple who'd gone walking hand in hand on the beach told a tale of wraiths crossing the road late at night, passing through the thick walls of the west tower, continuing onto the beach, and disappearing at the shoreline. "It was surreal," they said. "Like watching something from the past."

History

The East and West Martello Towers were each two stories high, but the staircase from the west tower was pillaged for the east tower and for Fort Taylor. In fact, that was how the crumbling fort became a horticultural marvel and prime tourist spot on Atlantic Boulevard.

Newly elected Representative Joe Allen was strolling along Higgs Beach when he passed prison laborers demolishing the west tower brick staircase. It was the 1980s, and locals disliked the ruins of the old west tower obscuring their view of the beach. But Representative Allen stopped the destruction and scouted for supporters. He found that the Key West Garden Club was interested, and West Martello Tower became its home.

The site eventually was christened the West Martello Tower Joe Allen Garden Center. According to a 1984 article in the *Key West Citizen*, "It will

Buddha in the bonsai tree area of the West Martello Tower Museum.

Saint Francis statue inside the West Martello Tower Museum.

probably be Rep. Allen's name that comes to mind when discussion centers around the garden center." Almost no one ever called it by that name, but Allen's effort speaks for itself. The brick walls are old and intricate and whole. The gardens are spectacular. There is a Prehistoric Garden, a Perfume Garden, a Butterfly Garden, and many rare and healthy species of plants. The west tower is also a popular wedding venue and the site of meetings and educational events. The West Martello Tower Museum is on the National Register of Historic Places.

ADDRESS:
WEST MARTELLO TOWER MUSEUM
110 ATLANTIC BOULEVARD, KEY WEST
305 294 3210

....

DEAN LOPEZ HORSE-DRAWN HEARSE

Things change.... Things happen....
Things you can't even imagine when you're young and full of hope.
—Judy Blume

GHOST STORY

The Dean Lopez Funeral Home was located on Bahama Street in the 1940s. It was there that almost seven thousand people crowded into a cramped room to view the corpse of Elena Milagro de Hoyos, who actually died ten years earlier.

The true crime story of Count Carl von Cosel and Elena Milagro de Hoyos is a lurid and morbid tale of obsession. The count was a German radiologist, and Elena was a young Cuban woman, married but deserted by her husband. Her mother brought her to the count for a chest X-ray. The count was married, but he'd abandoned his family. The minute he saw Elena, the count recognized her as the woman he'd seen all his life in his dreams. He was more than twice her age, and the examination yielded the

Dean Lopez Funeral Home today.

unhappy news that the young woman was suffering from tuberculosis. The count tried to cure her to no avail. She died in 1931. The count paid for her funeral and for her final resting place. For two years, he visited her every day at the Key West Cemetery. Then he lost his head completely, stole her body, and brought it to a wingless airplane he remodeled as a laboratory. Then he put her in a warehouse. He needed space, because this went on for years.

The count reconstructed Elena's body with rags, sewed on hair, used fabric to replace her decomposing skin, and gave her glass eyes. Eventually, Elena's sister caught on that something shocking was going on. She called the police, and Elena's corpse was taken to the Dean Lopez Funeral Home. The horrible history of the young women's desecration at the hands of a madman was labeled a "love story." Hordes of sightseers took in the spectacle of her oddly reconstructed remains.

The count spent the night in the old Monroe County jail. Authorities determined that the expiration of the statute of limitations provided a means of avoiding the count's prosecution. He was never punished. A friend put him up for a while, and then the crazed radiologist moved to Pasco County. He wrote a book. He became a U.S. citizen. Some people say he constructed a likeness of Elena out of wax and died with her in his arms.

The story of the count and his obsession is well known in Key West. It is the subject of many ghost tours and newspaper articles. Yet the story is only marginally connected to the Dean Lopez horse-drawn hearse because it is unlikely that Elena was transported from the count's clutches to the funeral home in that particular vehicle. However, a horse-drawn hearse is a classic and respectful way to transport the deceased. Somehow, it does seem appropriate to picture her in the fancy carriage, on her way, at last, to her final resting place.

History

The horse-drawn wooden hearse from the Dean Lopez Funeral Home was built in the late nineteenth century. Today, the Dean Lopez hearse is in bad shape: scuffed, worn, undrivable. In its heyday, its etchings, carved embellishments, and velvet curtains fringed with gold were some of the finer accoutrements of the mahogany vehicle.

The hearse transported dead sailors when the USS *Maine* exploded in 1898. Casualties of the consequent Spanish-American War rode in luxury to the Key West Cemetery. Most of all, it soothed grieving families by providing a dignified and solemn mode of transport for their deceased loved ones from home to the church and to the cemetery.

Dean Lopez horse-drawn hearse at Fort East Martello Tower Museum.

Plow horses were employed to haul the hearse. Usually, its passage was accompanied by a band of musicians and a coachman in top hat and tails. The formerly animal-powered vehicle made of wood, glass, and leather is available for viewing at the Fort East Martello Museum in the same room as Robert the Doll.

ADDRESS:
FORT EAST MARTELLO TOWER MUSEUM
3501 S ROOSEVELT BOULEVARD, KEY WEST
305 296 3913

....

FORT ZACHARY TAYLOR HISTORIC STATE PARK

A work in progress quickly becomes feral.
—Annie Dillard

GHOST STORY

Fort Zachary Taylor is the southernmost state park in the United States. From the salient angle of the fort's gun deck, one can see cruise ships loom in the distance and parasailers hover where the Atlantic Ocean meets the Gulf of Mexico. There is a beach nearby with picnic tables and occasional nude sunbathing. Its sunsets are spectacular. It is an idyllic setting for a fort named for a president who died in office and home of colorful invasive iguanas whom the natives hate and the tourists love.

The fort fits the bill for a haunted environment. It's 175-plus years old. There is some evidence that the grounds contain the remains of a city cemetery damaged by an 1836 hurricane. After the fort was built, there was a lot of death during the two wars (Civil and Spanish-American) during which it served, but not from battle. Soldiers died of yellow fever and were buried under the parade grounds. Traitors were shot. There was a military prison barracks where some tourists claim they still hear screams, mysterious gunfire, even whistles.

Above: Interior shot of Fort Taylor.

Opposite: Moat surrounding landlocked Fort Taylor.

According to eyewitnesses, there is a sentinel of Fort Taylor. Late at night, a mysterious figure stands near the fort's farthest exterior wall. This spectral sentinel scans the perimeter of the horizon, possibly protecting the fort from rebel forces. Is he a shadow from the Civil War, eternally performing his duties as a guard?

There are also tales of troops wearing uniforms from a variety of wars marshaling in the dead of night when it is stormy. And since executions in the past were performed at high noon for soldiers unlucky or stupid enough to desert and get caught, there are tales of hearing the creaking sound of the gallows trapdoor as it opens. Always at noon.

History

Construction on the fort was initiated in 1845, and Fort Taylor was completed in November 1850. In the interim, it was the only Key West edifice that stayed up through the hurricane of 1846. The man the fort honored with his name was President Zachary Taylor, known as Old Rough and Ready. But Taylor died before the grand opening from a stomach ailment, which may have been the result of scarfing a huge amount of ice cream at a Fourth of July celebration. He was dead by July 9, 1850.

From the air, Fort Taylor is trapezoid-shaped, made of brick, with a foundation of limestone and granite. It was built to protect the harbor, but today, because of the accumulation of sand, it is surrounded by land.

Its thick walls encase two levels of gun placements. Fort Zachary Taylor defended the southeast coast of the United States from attack by European entities. Known as the Gibraltar of the Gulf, its fifty acres were secured by the government to help the Union's naval blockade during the Civil War. Although it could accommodate almost one thousand soldiers, it was maintained by a few scores of Union combatants and never saw battle in

Opposite: One of the rare beaches in Key West at Fort Taylor State Park.

Above: A colorful iguana at Fort Taylor.

Right: Collection of cannons at Fort Taylor.

Latrines like the ones used by Union soldiers at Fort Taylor.

war. Its prisoners were blockade runners and deserters. Yet to this day, it stores the "largest collection of Civil War-era seacoast cannons in the U.S.," according to the fort's website.

Until the 1980s, no one could get into the fort because the navy held the surrounding land. Also, the whole Truman annex had to be completely restored, which took time and money. Today, Fort Taylor is managed by Florida Parks as a state park and a National Historic Landmark. Guided tours are offered.

Address:
Fort Zachary Taylor Historic State Park
601 Howard England Way
Southard Street on Truman Annex, Key West
305 292 6713

....

KEY WEST FIREHOUSE MUSEUM

They were talking about making it a parking garage.
Then they talked about condos.
—Alex Vega, retired fire chief

Ghost Story

If you watch the vlogs on YouTube, you'll see narrators tying most every Key West ghost story ever told to the four-thousand-square-foot two-story building on Grinnell Street. The Key West Firehouse Museum is such an easy target; it already has a reputation, and it embraces its historic paranormal rep like an old friend. For the curious, signs throughout the grounds announce the scheduled ghost tours of the "Haunted Firehouse." In spite of all the hoopla, which tends to breed doubt, this place probably is haunted.

It's not just the ghost of former fire chief Bum Farto, whose shady dealings with drugs ended the way most shady drug deal misunderstandings do. The quaintly named Key West denizen was known for his garish wardrobe, Cuban cigars, and reputation for idling around the firehouse (hence the

The Key West Firehouse Museum.

moniker Bum). After his conviction for selling cocaine and weed to an undercover narcotics agent, Bum disappeared in 1976 and was declared dead in the '80s. The firehouse was his refuge since boyhood. Why would Bum be anywhere else in death?

Volunteers report glowing orbs, moving objects, and full-body specters. Museum guide Mr. Collie claims that volunteers often hear footsteps on the second floor when no one is up there. They feel as though someone is watching them when no one is in the room. Small wonder.

Volunteers swear the antique fire truck in the yard is almost guaranteed to give those who enter an EVP (electronic voice phenomenon) along the lines of: "I'm here." The entity could be anyone. Visitors report hearing these words when citing the museum as one of the most haunted places in Key

Fire trucks where EVPs are often heard.

West. And paranormal investigators Messenger Paranormal found evidence of "unexplained phenomena," which allegedly convinced doubters of the firehouse's haunted status.

History

Built in 1907, Firehouse No. 3 is a museum, exhibiting original fire equipment, sleeping quarters, helmets, a fire pole, badges, and bells. Fire chief and drug dealer Bum Farto's original desk is still there. In the first quarter of the twentieth century, firehouses were small or housed in hotels. They were comprised of a small squadron of local volunteers, and many still used a horse-drawn wooden fire wagon. As cities grew, fire departments relocated to bigger buildings. In the case of Key West Firehouse No. 3, when everyone left, the building was left to deteriorate. By the 1990s, city officials wanted to tear it down.

That's when a retired fire chief, Alex Vega, started raising money through a nonprofit, applying for grants, and hounding locals for donations. Firefighters are American heroes, and firehouse history and preservation are popular with donors. Contributions poured in from all over the world, and today the museum does a lively business.

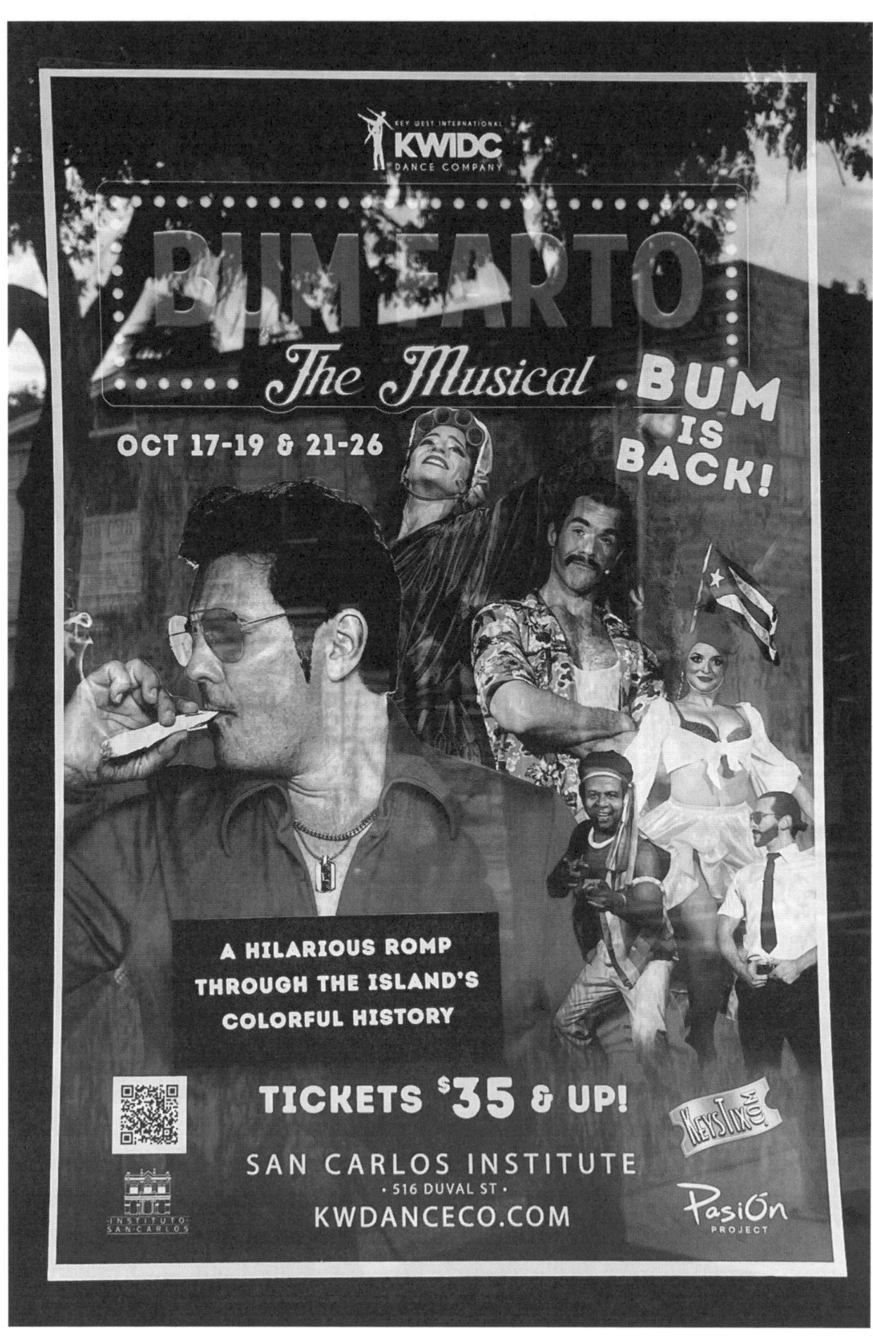

Ad for *Bum Farto the Musical*.

Vega wrote a book titled *The History of the Key West Firehouse No. 3*. It is available to purchase in the Firefighter's Lounge, where you can hang with retired firefighters and, supposedly, some of their ghosts. If that's not enough firefighter lore, the San Carlos Institute showcases a play in the fall titled *Bum Farto the Musical.* Appropriately, it coincides with Fantasy Fest.

ADDRESS:
KEY WEST FIREHOUSE MUSEUM
1025 GRINNELL STREET, KEY WEST
305 849 0678

....

HIGGS BEACH AFRICAN CEMETERY

Near this site lie the remains of 294 African men, women, and children who died in Key West in 1860.
—A Florida Heritage Landmark sponsored by Old Island Restoration Foundation and the Florida Department of State

GHOST STORY

There is a lot of paranormal activity on the beach named after a union boss and county commissioner. Clarence S. Higgs, who died in 1961, was concerned with bureaucracy, and it is not clear why a recreational site carries his name. Regardless, sixteen acres on the south side of the island are dedicated to local history, including the West Martello Tower (managed by the Key West Garden Club), the Key West AIDS Memorial, and the African Refugee Memorial. Beyond the African Refugee Memorial lies a series of unmarked graves near the beach walkway. There are more graves farther inland. This place is known as the African cemetery, the only one of its kind in America.

The African cemetery appears on an 1861 map drawn by the U.S. Army Corps of Engineers. Hundreds of West African refugees lost their lives from the desperate conditions aboard three slave ships bound for Cuba in 1860. The U.S. Navy commandeered the ships to Key West, a Union stronghold,

Left: Higgs Beach, where the community stepped in to save kidnapped and dying slaves.

Right: Tribute to the African cemetery next to the Casa Marina.

where the city took care of 1,500 sick, dying, and malnourished refugees for three months. Hundreds of the Africans, mostly children, died there of typhoid and dysentery.

Visitors claim that if you walk this beach at night, you will see the ghostly figures of the refugees searching for their families. You may hear whispers, shuffling footsteps in the sand, and weird sounds. Many researchers have experienced cold spots, a key indicator of a ghostly presence, later verified as actual graves located with ground-penetrating radar.

History

Although slavery was legal in the American South by the mid-nineteenth century, transporting kidnapped Africans procured by slave traders was not. According to the Mel Fisher Maritime Heritage Society in a study done in 2002:

> *During the spring and summer of 1860, the US Navy Steamers Mohawk, Wyandotte, and Crusader captured the American-owned slave ships Wildfire, William, and Bogota at various points near the Cuban coast. The ships were destined for the slave markets.*

African slaves were always targeted for dangerous agricultural functions, which are done by machinery today: cutting sugarcane, enduring toxic fumes from indigo dye, tending rice paddies, and, of course, picking cotton for hours under a Southern sun. The Africans aboard the captured slave ships were worth hard money to slave owners. Their duties constituted backbreaking labor, which, after the Civil War, plantation owners couldn't pay anyone to do.

The Africans aboard the *Bogota*, after suffering "only" twenty-four deaths, were deemed among the healthiest of the hostages and were eventually sold as slaves, although it is unclear who profited by the sales. Mortality and mortal illness among the refugees aboard the *Wildfire* and the *Williams* were rampant. Many of these sufferers did not survive the Middle Passage, or they survived just long enough to die on American soil. Some of the women on the slave ships gave birth en route in such squalid conditions that their babies did not survive.

Every year, Key West celebrates a festival called One Human Family, which promotes the deep social and spiritual values of Key West citizens past and present. In 1860, the city demonstrated those values when local people nursed, fed, and sheltered the African refugees rescued from the slave ships on a Key West beach. The surviving refugees aboard two of the ships were later relocated to Liberia, a colony founded in 1819 by political leaders and the American Colonization Society. Then history loses track of them.

In 2002, the public of Key West discovered their local beach was a gigantic grave site, although this was scarcely a secret. The graves were documented by the Army Corps of Engineers in the nineteenth century, and skeletons were excavated during the construction of the West Martello Tower. A memorial was established to honor the lives of the kidnapped refugees who perished. A representative of the refugees' tribe performed a grave site ceremony. On March 22, 2020, Key West commemorated the "International Day of Remembrance for the Victims of Slavery and the

Memorial to victims of the slave trade buried on the beach.

Transatlantic Slave Trade" at the African Refugee Memorial. For more information, contact the Mel Fisher Maritime Museum on Greene Street, which has an exhibit of relics, maps, and historical data about the grave site.

The Clarence S. Higgs Memorial Beach Park's African Cemetery is listed on the National Register of Historic Places.

Address:
African Cemetery
Clarence S. Higgs Memorial Beach Park
1074–1094 Atlantic Boulevard, Key West

....

Historic Key West Cemetery

I wish to be buried at sea between Key West and Cuba,
dropped overboard in a clean white sack.
—Tennessee Williams, who was buried in St. Louis, a city he loathed

Ghost Story

In the nineteenth century, cemeteries commonly grew up around isolated headstones. The Key West Cemetery is no exception, with headstones from the 1820s that predate the cemetery. The nineteen-acre graveyard on Passover Lane was employed as a graveyard in 1847, years after a hurricane swept away bodies in another cemetery on the beach somewhere between Fort Taylor and the West Martello Tower. There are haunting accounts of caskets strewn among the mangroves or floating down streets.

Today, the Historic Key West Cemetery is famous for its spooky reputation. There are reports by paranormal investigators of ghostly animals who growl or purr on EVP detectors. There are cold spots and flashes of orbs, they say. If you sit on a grave or grind a cigarette into the ground, there is a possibility a female ghost with a Bahamian accent will scold and even try to push you. The spirits from the USS *Maine* wander about, walking through the memorial that honors them in death. Yellow fever fatalities fall into ghostly seizures. A lynched World War I veteran stands guard at the gate.

The cemetery is known as the City of the Dead.

The Cuban compatriots of José Marti congregate, hobnobbing in the stark city of the dead.

Widowed Enriquetta (nickname Hetty) Marrero, thrown out of her home on Fleming Street by her late husband's first wife, divides her time between her former home, now a small, stylish hotel, and the graveyard where she trips up visitors to her husband's grave.

There are even sightings of a trenchcoated Tennessee Williams brooding in the moonlight. His brother buried him in St. Louis, a place to which he never wanted to return. Perhaps he followed his heart and escaped to the city he loved.

History

Although the Key West cemetery is supposed to be the highest and driest point on the island (sixteen feet above sea level), it holds mostly aboveground burials. As in the cemeteries in New Orleans, a storm surge can push coffins up out of their graves, which happened pretty routinely after hurricanes. And as in the cemeteries of New Orleans, there are more dead on the island than living; seventy thousand bodies are accounted for on this narrow strip of coral. Less than twenty-five thousand people actually live in Key West. There are scores of unreported grave sites throughout the city and the Keys.

One of the most famous grave sites belongs to Sloppy Joe Russell, a boat captain, bootlegger, fisherman, saloonkeeper, and character literally straight out of a Hemingway novel. Always on the edge of the law, he ran speakeasies during Prohibition. He was the founder of a bar in Cuba where he went by the name of José. His friends berated him for the messy appearance of his establishment and began calling him Sloppy Joe. In 1933, Joe opened Sloppy Joe's Bar in Key West, which was located on Greene Street at the present-day Captain Tony's saloon. It stands to reason Joe was a close friend of Ernest Hemingway, who even used him as the basis of the fictional barkeep in his novel *To Have and Have Not*. Joe died in his fifties, in 1941, of a heart attack.

Key West is an integrated cemetery containing cigar makers, people of divergent religions and races, and soldiers. Elena Milagro de Hoyos, the obsession of the lunatic Count Cosel, is, fittingly, in an unmarked grave.

There is a monument to the naval crew of the USS *Maine*, which blew up in Havana and started the Spanish-American War. Ironically, there are theories that it was not a mine or a submarine that sank the ship. Experts today hypothesize that the explosion may have been caused by a coal ember triggering the ship's explosives.

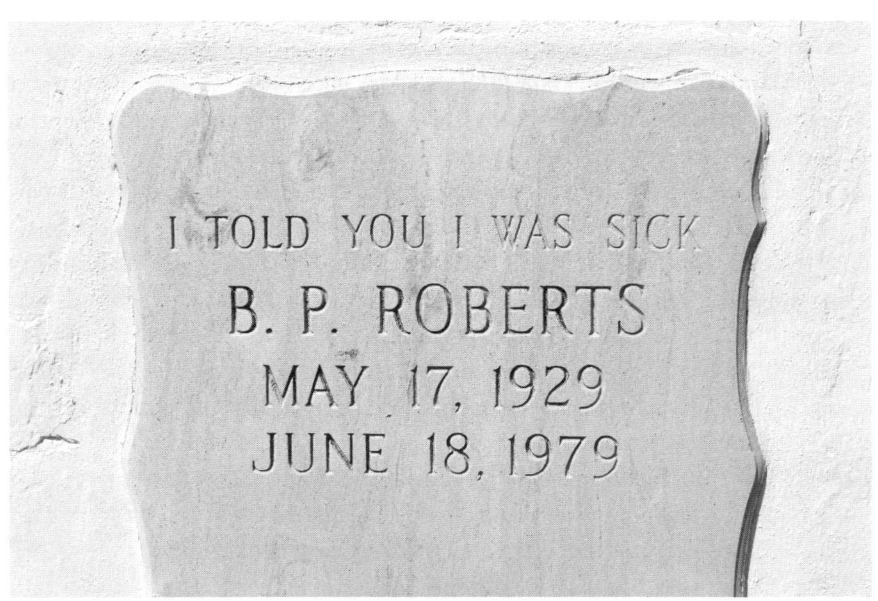

Opposite: USS *Maine* memorial at the Key West Cemetery.

Above: Quirky inscription at the Key West Cemetery.

Right: An old conch in the graveyard.

At one time, the cemetery was closed to new entombments, but it expanded about five acres and resumed business. One hundred people a year choose this cemetery as their final resting place. Pets are buried here as well. More than one Yorkie and a German shepherd rest in peace among the headstones. Even a deer is buried here, although it is unknown if it was a pet or roadkill.

The Key West Cemetery is approaching the containment of one hundred thousand souls. Some had a dry sense of humor. B.P. Roberts, who died at the age of fifty in 1979, had "I told you I was sick" inscribed above his name. Gloria Russell admonishes onlookers, "I'm just resting my eyes." A giant conch shell no doubt reflects the passing of a native Key Wester.

Address:
Historic Key West Cemetery
701 Passover Lane, Key West
305 809 3986

....

St. Paul's Episcopal Church Cemetery

We came to kick in the door.
—The Fabulous Spectrelles, who performed at St. Paul's Church in the '80s

Ghost Story

For those lucky enough to stake a plot in Key West, St. Paul's Episcopal Church on Duval Street sponsored a small cemetery and a memorial garden behind the church. This cemetery has graves and cremated remains from the antebellum period of Florida history. John Fleming's widow donated the land for the church and cemetery in 1832 on the condition that they didn't disturb her husband's remains. It appears that Fleming, a Key West founder, also haunts the grounds. His final resting place is a mystery.

St. Paul's Episcopal Church on Duval Street.

Left: Six people are buried under the Episcopal church.

Below: An unexplained streak of light among the ashes behind St. Paul's Episcopal church.

A rear view of St. Paul's cemetery.

Several visitors report seeing a man wearing a tailcoat and a tall beaver hat striding up and down the aisles in a perpetual fog. Although Fleming lived in Massachusetts, he struck a deal with the other founding fathers (John Whitehead, John Simonton, and Pardon Green) to divvy up the land on the narrow coral and limestone rock. Fleming took ten years to come up with an economic plan, largely concerning salt mining, but when he returned to Key West, he died. His cause of death is unknown, and his exact grave site is not marked, perhaps because there have been so many reconstructions and renovations of the church.

Other specters include a sea captain who materializes from time to time. A spirit who rid the island of pirates sends a gale-force wind rattling the limbs of a tree near his grave. The virulence of an arsonist's attempt to get back at his adulterous wife (see the section "Key West Theater") left several children trapped in a fiery blaze. Visitors hear children's voices, especially near an angel near the corner of the cemetery.

History

The church was built in 1838 of coral rock and destroyed ten years later by a hurricane. Forty years after being rebuilt with wood, the church was

An interior view of St. Paul's.

demolished in the Great Fire of Key West. St. Paul's was rebuilt again with wood—a bad choice—and twenty years later, a hurricane leveled it again. Rebuilt once more, this time from concrete, the church is a magnificent structure, its tiles devised by a Key West artist and church member. The artist was Robert Gene Otto, who lived in the Artist House and owned the notorious Robert the Doll. The church was refurbished again in the 1990s, when the concrete walls started to crack from seawater corrosion. Twentieth-century artists designed the stained-glass windows.

Aside from its fraught survival, St. Paul's is famous for its ten bells, installed in 1891, which used to chime twice a day for fifteen minutes. The largest bell weighs almost a ton. All bells have been muted for years because of hurricane damage to the bell tower, and some of them are cracked. The church is working on repairs with grant money.

St. Paul's is also well known for its stained-glass artistry of religious themes and Key West history. A book was written in 2007 by a parishioner, Winifred Shine Fryzel, titled *The Golden Cockerel: The Art, Symbolism & History of the Stained Glass Windows, St. Paul's Episcopal Church, Key West, Florida*. It is out of print, but portions of the manuscript are available on the church's website.

St. Paul's Episcopal Church in Key West is recognized as a historic site and is affiliated with the National Fund for Sacred Places.

Address:
St. Paul's Episcopal Church Cemetery
401 Duval Street, Key West
305 296 5142

....

San Carlos Institute

Those who do not learn from history are doomed to repeat it.
—José Marti

Ghost Story

In 1892, Cuba's national hero José Marti met comrades at the San Carlos Institute to organize the Cuban revolutionary army against Spain's military dictator, General Batista. It is said that Marti's spirit lingers in the building built by Cuban exiles and funded with their wages as cigar makers. These spirits are not alone. This island performance hall on Duval Street experiences more than its share of strange occurrences and ghost stories.

There are the usual apparitions, cold spots, and unexplained noises, including gunshots. In 1981, a tourist stopped under its eaves to light a cigarette, and a tile fell on his head, beaning him. Then there is the story of a man who, incensed over the leadership of the institute, smashed a window. He died in a peculiar way four years later.

The spirit of Armando Alejandre Jr., a member of Brothers to the Rescue, is said to haunt the premises. According to the *Key West Citizen*, Alejandre was "on a humanitarian search and rescue mission over the Florida Straits for Cuban rafters in international airspace." The civilian plane was shot down by the Cuban air force in 1996.

It would be too harsh an afterlife for Alejandre Jr., who hated Castro, to haunt the communist island. However, the San Carlos Institute is a home away from home. Besides, José Marti needs volunteers for his ghostly group of rebels.

The San Carlos Institute.

HISTORY

The San Carlos Institute was named after a college in Cuba and after a wealthy Cuban patriot, Carlos Manuel de Céspedes. By the 1980s, however, the building was nearly decrepit. It was refurbished, and today the two-story structure integrates the charm of Cuban architecture. The ceilings are high, and there are stone staircases, arched doorways, wrought iron balconies, mosaics, and terra-cotta glazed tile.

Managed by the San Carlos Institute, the building is occupied by a museum, a school, and a theater. At one time it was a Cuban consulate and a meeting ground for Cuban revolutionaries planning to take their independence from Spain. Today, members of Congress are sworn in here. Teenage girls celebrate their quinceañeras in the fashion of debutante balls.

Yet the building's existence is under existential threat because its ownership is questionable. This is nothing new in Key West, where various land claims and fraudulent land sales prevailed before Simonton, Greene, Whitehead, and Fleming divided Key West between them. But the reality of a communist foreign government owning property in an American city is another matter entirely.

The government of Cuba and the institute in Key West grappled with this issue for decades. Cuba is the actual trustee of the property, but the institute, which runs and maintains it, claims it has rights as the "beneficial owner." To make matters more complicated, there is a third-party lawsuit at stake by a woman petitioning for compensation from the United States and Cuba over the torture and execution of her father at the hands of the Cuban rebels and their allies (Eisenhower supported the rebels). She seeks $63 million in compensation.

How likely is it that the lawsuit, which is twenty-two years old, will prevail? If it does, the plaintiff may sell San Carlos for a few million dollars. With it will go the "Jewel of Duval Street" and an important conveyor of Cuban history, art, and culture. At the same time, it is fascinating that there is a structure in Key West with a rich Cuban heritage that may be lost to commercial interests because of a casualty in a revolution that occurred eighty years ago.

The San Carlos Institute is on the National Register of Historic Places.

Address:
San Carlos Institute
516 Duval Street, Key West

....

CAPTAIN TONY'S SALOON

All you need in this life is a tremendous sex drive and a great ego. Brains don't mean [expletive].
—Tony Tarracino (Captain Tony)

Ghost Story

Since Captain Tony's Saloon was a morgue in the nineteenth century, there are bodies buried under the floorboards and beneath the draped bras adorning the crumbling Hanging Tree where at least thirteen pirates and many murderers met their maker.

Left: The original Sloppy Joe's.

Below: The skeleton of an Indian princess taken from a shipwreck.

Staff affirm that doors lock and unlock, voices call "Don't leave," and a lady in bloodstained blue materializes near cold spots. The Lady in Blue chopped up her husband and two sons with an axe in the nineteenth century, and she was dispatched to the Hanging Tree in short order. The Hanging Tree is said have been a live oak growing inside the bar. It is coated with some kind of resin, and the upper branches are broken. Back in the day, it was used for public executions. Suffice to say that the spirits of murderers and pirates that permeate the bar are anything but friendly. And suffice to say that tipplers on a Key West spree know enough to stop drinking when these cutthroats materialize.

History

Captain Tony's Saloon, like its namesake, tried on many different identities. It was a telegraph office, a brothel, an icehouse, and a morgue. It was the original Sloppy Joe's. In 1933, the owner raised the rent, and Sloppy Joe Russell moved his bar across the street to Duval in the middle of the night. For a while, the old Sloppy Joe's was a gay bar called the Duval Club and then a speakeasy known as the Blind Pig.

Tony Tarracino, the bar's irascible owner and namesake, was more of a bootlegger and gunrunner than a captain, and his colorful character is still legend in Key West. Born in New Jersey—and maintaining a strong Jersey accent throughout his life—he bought the saloon in 1961. By the late '80s, Tarracino had become, improbably, the mayor of Key West, embracing the idea of Key West seceding from the United States and becoming a free state called the Conch Republic. Embodying the Key West lifestyle, Tarracino married four times and fathered thirteen children, the youngest when he was seventy years old. His last wife, Marty, almost fifty years younger than the charismatic captain, was with Tarracino when he died in the Lower Keys Medical Center in 2008.

Entering Captain Tony's saloon is an eye-opening experience unless you are very drunk, which many of its patrons consider the only way to approach the grungy century-old watering hole. Its walls are black, and there is a tree trunk hung with lingerie; a preserved jewfish, Goliath, over the sign (tourists try to throw coins into its open jaw for luck); and a human skeleton hanging behind the bar (Tarracino used to say she was a Spanish princess he found near a shipwreck).

Shel Silverstein with Captain Tony. *Photo by Rob O'Neal.*

This is pretty much the way the bar looked for decades except for the pool tables and pinball machines, which replaced the card and craps tables. The ceiling fans whir, the doors are wide open, sawdust is on the floor, a long wooden bar flanks both sides of the register, and barstools bearing the names of such famous patrons as Tennessee Williams (who liked to frequent the bar wearing a trench coat and nothing else), Truman Capote (who notably offered to write his initials on the exposed member of a flashing patron), Hemingway (a drunk and a loner, according to Tarracino), and Jimmy Buffett (whose song "Last Mango in Paris" mentions Tarracino).

Enlarged black-and-white photos of Tarracino, Buffett, and Shel Silverstein hang amid the license plates, dollar bills, and bras on the walls. There are still live performances on the saloon's open stage featuring musicians singing a lively version of "Who Put the Pepper in the Vaseline?" among other favorites. This is old Key West—lock, stock, and saloon.

Address:
Captain Tony's Saloon
428 Green Street, Key West

. . . .

KEY WEST LIGHTHOUSE MUSEUM

Even though the lighthouse had seen better days, the sheer strength of it was still very much apparent. I just stood there and stared up, wondering how in the hell they'd built it.
—Jimmy Buffett as the character Tully Mars
in his book A Salty Piece of Land

Ghost Story

The Key West lighthouse is almost certainly haunted by former lighthouse keeper Barbara Mabrity. Her husband, Michael, was the first lighthouse tender, and when he died, Barbara took on his responsibilities. She served for thirty-two years. During that time, a traumatic event occurred.

The Havana hurricane of 1846 roared southwest fifteen years into Mabrity's tenure. The high winds and sea eventually destroyed the lighthouse, although Mabrity kept the light on as long as possible. She survived, but six of her children were taken by the waves.

Lighthouse pie drop contest, Fourth of July.

Mabrity resolved not to let such a weighty sacrifice go in vain. Dedicated to her important role as the keeper of the light, she worked until her eighties. Then she was fired for her anti-Union remarks during the Civil War. Key West was a Southern city, but Union forces controlled the island.

Mabrity could not have taken her forced resignation well. It is said that her soul never left the grounds of the lighthouse. Even though she and her children have been gone for ages, people say that during storms, they can hear their spirits screaming in the wind as the hurricane blows them farther and farther into the sea.

HISTORY

In the eighteenth and nineteenth centuries, Key West residents appropriated the Bahamians' business and made their livings as wreckers, salvaging and pillaging boats that ran aground or crashed in the shallow, rocky coastline. Shipbuilders opposed this profession, insisting the government provide routing devices for the dangerous one-hundred-mile coral barrier reef. The Key West lighthouse, built in 1848, was the result.

As is usual on Florida coastlines, another lighthouse preceded the present one. The hurricane of 1846 destroyed it, but the consequent beacon of safety was finished in two years more inland and on higher ground to protect it from flooding. A Fresnel lens followed a decade later. Over time, as Key West developed, the area around the lighthouse accrued sand, leaving it surrounded by land not the sea.

At seventy-three feet, the Key West lighthouse is half the size and half the amount of steps of the St. Augustine lighthouse. Yet, it functioned as a working beacon light, steering ships to safety in the night for over one hundred years. It was retired in the late 1960s.

Now the lighthouse structure is a relic, and the lighthouse keeper's quarters are a museum. Including vintage photos of the lighthouse construction, the living quarters contain the original furniture such as oil lamps, porcelain, and chamber pots. It is still a popular tourist spot, and locals get in on the antics as well.

On July Fourth, a popular attraction known as the Key Lime Pie Drop occurs. The point is to drop the pie almost one hundred feet to the ground without smashing the Key West delicacy. Some tossers use tiny parachutes attached to the pie to accomplish the feat. The winner takes home a prize, but it's unclear if it's pie in the sky.

Also available as a wedding venue, the Key West Lighthouse is a National Historic Landmark. It is managed by the Key West Art & Historical Society.

Address:
Key West Lighthouse
938 Whitehead Street, Key West

. . . .

KEY WEST SHIPWRECK TREASURES MUSEUM

People don't choose their careers; they are engulfed by them.
—John Dos Passos

Ghost Story

The shipwreck museum is supposed to be one of the most haunted places in Key West, and visitors and staff have reported apparitions, cold spots, and EVPs. Some paranormal interpreters speculate that the items in the museum itself are haunted, retaining intangible imprints from centuries-old owners.

At least one thousand shipwrecks are still strewn along the Keys coastline—one hundred of them in Key West alone. Initial salvagers did not have the benefit of scuba tanks or gear. They went down thirty feet holding their breath with a rope tied around their waist. Divers found treasure by groping with their hands, tying the artifacts to the rope, and tugging to indicate they were ready to be lifted out of the water. Deck crews held the ropes tightened to their limit in order to lift heavy, unwieldy goods. Many of the hired salvagers perished in one way or another. The loot displayed in the museum should reflect their sacrifice, if not their supernatural presence.

Certainly the story of the "cursed" silver bar bears some scrutiny. The museum mostly contains the relics of the 137-foot three-masted schooner the *Isaac Allerton*. But there are some pieces from the Spanish galleon *Nuestra Señora de las Maravillas* as well. The *Maravillas* collided with another ship in 1656, smashed into a coral reef, and sank in the Bahamas. Hundreds of people died in that shipwreck, mostly drowned or eaten by sharks.

The Key West shipwreck museum with lookout tower.

The *Maravillas* carried personal treasure as well as salvage from the shipwreck of the *Jesús María de la Limpia Concepción*, which sank in 1654. In the ensuing years, two other ships carrying salvaged treasure from the *Concepción* and the *Maravilla* also foundered. The "cursed" silver bar in the museum, which is almost identical to a silver bar in the Old St. Augustine History Museum, was presumably recovered from one of the wrecks. Both museums invite you to try to lift the silver bars.

Other ghostly encounters may involve the spirit of a thirty-one-year-old Orlando man who died by suicide on the lookout tower of the museum in 2008. The man perished by a self-inflicted gunshot from a 9 mm handgun to his head. Bob Eadie, a Monroe County Health Department administrator, says Monroe County has "the highest suicide rate among all sixty-seven Florida counties." His estimate must include tourists as well.

There were two alarms on the tower, and on that fateful day in 2008 they both went off in the wee hours of the morning. Apparently the museum's private security guards showed up but did not climb the tower. The body was not discovered until later that morning, along with the handgun and a cell phone. If in death people pick up where they left off in life, that unfortunate man's spirit may well continue hanging around the tower, unsure if he is really dead.

History

The original shipwreck museum was known as the Historic Key West Shipwreck Museum. It was opened by Ray and Steve Maloney and Monroe County Commissioner Doug Jones. The Maloneys are descendants of the original wreckers' lawyer, Walter Maloney (who also published the first written history of the island, "A Sketch of the History of Key West, 1876").

The Maloneys and the Joneses ran the museum on the ground floor of the old city hall on Green Street. Their display was mostly artifacts from the hurricane-ravaged shipwreck *Isaac Allerton*, "buried in the mud near Hawk's Channel," which sank in 1856. The Maloney duo salvaged it in 1985. The mud kept the artifacts intact.

The shipwreck museum opened in 1989, but it was open for only a few years when a fierce rent dispute between the city and the Maloneys drove the brothers from their spot in city hall. For a while, the relocated museum was known as Key West Shipwreck Historeum. Now the salvaged treasures reside in an old reconstructed warehouse on the grounds of Mallory Square, built to look like the warehouse of wrecker Asa Tift. (Tift was also a builder: He built Hemingway's eventual Key West abode in the nineteenth century.)

Most of what was found by salvagers is on display today at the Key West Treasure and Shipwreck Museum, with two floors of wreckage swag and interactive displays. This includes coins, plates, pewterware, jewelry, tools, wine bottles, a piece of marble, and some apparel. The museum also shows educational films and employs docents in traditional nineteenth-century attire.

There is a sixty-five-foot tower to climb, Key West's tallest lookout, which gives tourists an idea of how the wreckers studied the reef for a "wreck ashore." The view, enhanced by a telescope, displays the city of Key West and the coral reefs. Unless a big commercial cruise ship blocks the sight of the horizon, that vista alone is worth the price of admission.

ADDRESS:
KEY WEST SHIPWRECK TREASURES MUSEUM
1 WHITEHEAD STREET, KEY WEST
305 292 8990

....

KEY WEST THEATER

I visited this place on a ghost tour back in 2004. My friends and I all felt an eerie heat standing next to the building as if it was burning. What was crazy was as the tour guide started explaining the building had in fact burned down (several times), the sensation stopped. It was crazy!
—2022 review on Yelp

GHOST STORY

Ghosts like large buildings with plenty of open space where they can linger unimpeded, places like churches and theaters. Fortunately for the ghosts of 512 Eaton Street, the site of the Key West Theater has provided both.

In 1848, the Eaton Street address identified the Key West First Baptist Church, where, apparently, no one was immune to the temptations of the

The Key West Theater today.

flesh: The minister's wife was carrying on with the deacon, and everyone in town knew it. The minister stood it for six months. Then, spying the couple embracing on the hard Baptist pews, he snapped. He splashed kerosene around the grounds of the holy place, locked all the doors, and lit a match.

The adulterers burned, along with about seventeen children who had just arrived for choir practice. People in the street say they sometimes hear screams coming from the theater. It is hard to know who haunts the Key West Theater: the minister, the wife, the deacon, or the children. On ghost tours, the host often asks ticket holders to huddle under the marquee and listen.

"What're we listening for?" someone inevitably asks.

"Tapping," the tour leader says.

"Tapping? Who's tapping?"

"The children," the tour leader says. "They're still trying to get out."

History

After the church burned down, another church was built on the property and then was converted to a theater. That didn't go too well. If a someone lit a cigarette, objects would get thrown around without a discernable presence. Construction workers wouldn't stay because of all the paranormal activity. It was a dance club for a while, Club Chameleon, but patrons smelled smoke when there was no fire and heard voices. The club stood vacant for several years.

It seems the curse of the location has finally been lifted, if the Key West Theater is any indication. The nonprofit has an impressive list of upcoming events, including several cover bands, Garrison Keillor of *Prairie Home Companion* fame, and an "R-rated hypnotist." The theater won the Key West People's Choice Award for five consecutive years from 2016 to 2024. The beige, blue, and maroon building also rents rooms as meeting venues, and there is a recording studio consisting of a tracking room, control room, and rehearsal room. The only smoke that's been reported lately is from the hot licks of rock and jazz music.

Address:
Key West Theater
512 Eaton Street, Key West
305 985 0433

....

OLD MONROE COUNTY JAIL

Past the back of the brick courthouse with its clock luminous at half-past ten, past the whitewashed jail building shining in the moonlight.
—*Ernest Hemingway,* The Sun Also Rises

Ghost Story

An infamous lynching in 1921 involved a native Key Wester and army veteran, Manuel Cabeza. He lived with a woman of mixed Cuban and

The Old Monroe County jail on Jackson Square.

African descent, and his lack of regard for Jim Crow laws infuriated members of the Ku Klux Klan, who consequently tarred and feathered him. Cabeza recognized his attackers in spite of the white hoods and took a shot at one of them, a manager of a cigar factory. The man died.

There was no denying what Cabeza had done, and the veteran was taken into custody at the old Monroe County jail and guarded in his cell by marines. However, the same night Carbeza was arrested, the Monroe County sheriff told the marines to go home. Carloads of Klansmen, who had infiltrated the police force, materialized shortly thereafter. Cabeza was seized from the jail, beaten, dragged by a car, lynched, and shot. As usual in such cases, no one was ever charged with the murder, let alone tried.

However, legend has it that the girlfriend, Angela, performed magic rituals after her lover's brutal murder. It is said that every Klan member who participated in Cabeza's killing died from unexplained and unexpected accidents in the following years.

Cabeza's ghost still haunts the old jail. He doesn't speak, but witnesses have seen his pale face, his eyes big, as he peers out, listens, and holds on tight to the bars.

History

There have been so many Monroe County jails, they are hard to count. The first jail was wood frame and "quite distant from the settled part of town." In 1835, a stone jail was built, and then another. By 1892, five jails had been either torn down, blown down, or caught on fire. Construction materials of imported red brick were ferried to the island and used to erect the jail on Jackson Square next to the courthouse. It was similar to the courthouse in design and in a convenient location to herd prisoners straight from court into cells. Fifteen years later, a ten-foot concrete wall went up around the rear of the jail, which is still there today.

There were usually less than a dozen prisoners, mostly young, all men, some local, some Bahamian. Prisoners who were sentenced to death were hanged in the rear yard of the jail (maybe another reason for the wall). These were public executions, which went on until 1904. The jail's most famous prisoner was Carl Tanzler, the twentieth-century German scientist who desecrated the body of Elena Milagro de Hoyos (see the section "Dean

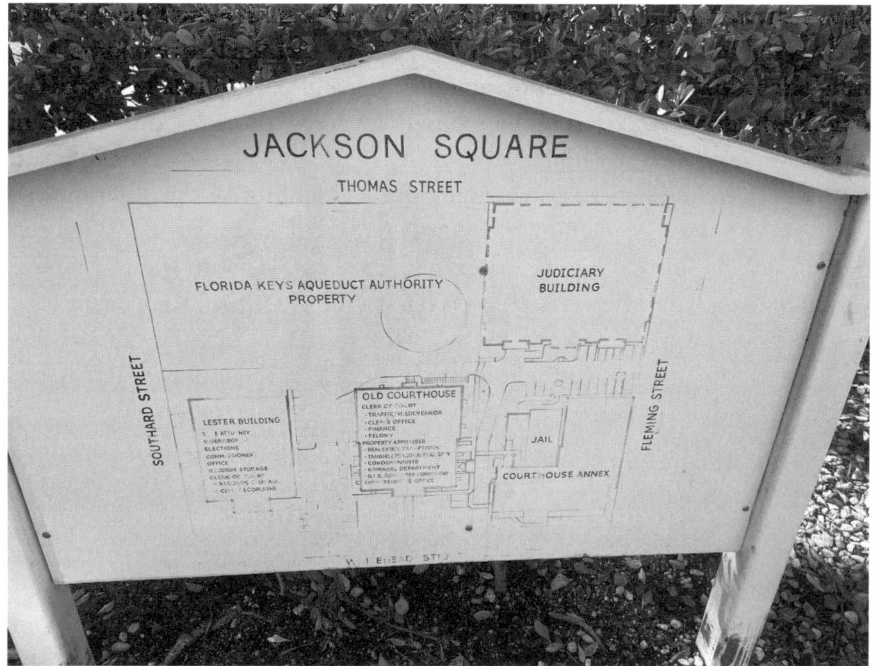

Map of Jackson Square.

Kiosk at the old jail.

Lopez Horse-Drawn Hearse"). He was held in the old Monroe County jail for a short time.

The old Monroe County jail is being renovated as a museum. The museum was supposed to open in 2023, and the bulk of the renovations are supposedly done. Dan Price, director of retail for the museum, says he has products lined up for the museum stores. As of this writing, the Monroe County Board of County Commissioners is expected to take up the matter of the old Monroe County jail and its museum status in 2025.

When asked whether the project was still in the works, project manager Cary Vicks wrote in an email, "The short answer is yes, but it is not open to the public yet. We are working to formalize a lease with the Key West Arts and Historical Society to operate and maintain the historical jail as a museum." Today the old jail displays an Historic Key West Marker as part of a virtual walking tour in conjunction with the Key West Art and Historical Society.

There is yet another Monroe County detention center, this one on Stock Island in the Lower Keys. It was completed in 1993.

Address:
Key West Old Jail
Whitehead Street, 500 Block
(looking south from the courthouse)
Key West

Key West Historic Marker
322 Fleming Street, Key West
For a free audio walking tour, call: 305 507 0300

....

KEY WEST MUSEUM OF ART AND HISTORY AT THE CUSTOM HOUSE

I am able to see what the artist originally missed.
—Seward Johnson

GHOST STORY

There are many ghost stories floating around the Custom House. Some claim that during the 1993 renovation, construction workers kept finding their tools in places other than where they'd left them. There were shadowy figures spotted, cold spots, unexplained creaks, footsteps, and groans.

One unusual ghostly story came from a tourist who was sitting outside the museum on a bench while her husband purchased their tickets. She said she must have passed out, and when she came to, her husband was shaking her.

"I don't know what came over me," the tourist said. "But something did. I saw myself floating over the roof. I saw steamer ships unloading and people passing cargo hand over hand, up and down the pier. When I came back to my body, there was a man sitting beside me. He wore an old-fashioned uniform. He didn't say anything. Then I came to."

Whether the tourist's out-of-body experience was genuine or not, no one can say. But there are reports of a nineteenth-century customs official who was murdered in the building. Perhaps his ghost was getting some fresh air.

HISTORY

The island of Key West enjoyed several vantage points, which inspired some nineteenth-century lawmakers and merchants to call it the "Commercial Emporium of the State of Florida." The first advantage was its physical location as the southernmost point in the contiguous United States.

It takes a long time to travel around the Florida peninsula, which is why developers and the government tried to cut Florida in half more than once to establish a barge canal. But Key West was close to and could easily trade with some foreign countries. And Key West could export whatever it happened to be selling at the time: cigars, fish, pineapples, sponges, salt.

Key West's generously deep harbors were perfect for shipments in or out. Thus was the first Key West customhouse established in a tiny wooden

The Key West Museum of Art and History at the Custom House.

Left: Hemingway at the Old Custom House.

Opposite: Seward's *Time for Fun. Photo by Elizabeth Randall.*

structure that opened in 1833. A staff was hired: customhouse officers, collectors, coast guard authorities. According to *A Sketch of the History of Key West* by Walter C. Maloney, as early as 1828, Key West was declared the "Port of Entry to Florida"—and, in many cases, to the world. Half a century later, the customhouse in Key West was generating greater profits than all other Florida ports.

From 1831 to 1835, imports that came through the customhouse, including foreign shipments, were worth considerably more than Key West exports. In addition, problematic trade policies toward Spain and England made it almost impossible to internationally barter without breaking some law or other. Magistrates and judges were in a quandary about what to do with people caught with illegal imports. Many looked the other way. This may have had something to with slave ships coming from foreign countries, which were outlawed in 1807. The first customhouse processed slave ships even though such vessels, and their human cargo, constituted an act of piracy. The population of slaves in Key West grew exponentially from 1850 to 1860.

Notwithstanding these difficulties and moral challenges, the customhouse flourished. According to the Custom Book records, by 1876, Key West's port of entry dominated collection along the southern coast all the way up to Charleston, South Carolina. The customhouse generated almost $300,000 that year in duties and dues. This successful industry led to the completion of the structure we know today. In 1891, the massive redbrick building presently presiding over Front Street was built as a customhouse, post office, federal courthouse, and the Seventh District Lighthouse Offices.

Yet customs profits ceased during the Great Depression, and the navy took over the building. After a decade, they left too. The building was vacant for a long time until the Key West Art and Historical Society spent $9 million restoring and refurbishing it. Today, it is the historical society's official headquarters, featuring two floors of exhibits, including Guy Harvey sketches illustrating Hemingway's *The Old Man and the Sea*. There are numerous exhibitions displaying the history of Key West and its citizens: the sinking of the USS *Maine*, Henry Flagler's Overseas Railroad, the hurricane of 1935, and Works Progress Administration art. Native Key Wester Mario Sanchez has an exhibition of painted wood carvings depicting the diversity of Key West culture. Artifacts of Ernest Hemingway's and Tennessee Williams's work are displayed as well.

Designed by William Kerr in the Romanesque Revival form, the large redbrick building has functioned as a museum inside and out. During the 1990s, and as recently as 2017, Seward Johnson, an artist, sculpted giant painted bronze statues that were displayed outside the Key West customhouse. One of the notable sculptures was a fifteen-thousand-pound couple dancing, which was modeled after a Renoir painting, called *Time for Fun*. Johnson's sculptures were often displayed on and off around the customhouse, but it is uncertain if they will appear again. Seward died in 2020.

The customhouse in Key West is listed on the National Register of Historic Places.

ADDRESS:
THE OLD CUSTOM HOUSE
281 FRONT STREET, KEY WEST
305 295 6616

....

EATON LODGE/OLD TOWN MANOR

Key West, for me, was a tropical island paradise.
—Gloria Swanson

GHOST STORY

Formerly known as the Eaton Lodge, the Old Town Manor is a fully refurbished Victorian/Greek Revival bed-and-breakfast haunted with a poignant love story. The ghosts, Mrs. and Dr. William Richard Warren, are anything but intimidating.

The Eaton Lodge is now the Old Town Manor.

Dr. Warren and his bride, Genevieve Allen, were natives of Key West. While there is no direct evidence that Dr. William Richard Warren was a descendant of Richard Warren of *Mayflower* fame, the similarity in name and proximity bear further research. The *Mayflower* passenger holds the distinction of having "the most descendants in Florida."

Whatever Dr. Warren's lineage consisted of, there was no doubt that Genevieve was from an old and prominent Key West family. Her parents bought the house on Eaton Street as a wedding present when she married Dr. Warren in 1913. He practiced medicine from their home, which he later enlarged and added on to. His wife created an ornamental garden featuring palm trees and orchids, among other exotic plants, and she is honored in perpetuity by the Key West Garden Club.

By all accounts, they were a happy, professional, community-minded couple who loved entertaining. And perhaps they were reluctant to leave even in death. Guests and staff describe hearing footsteps on the stairs and the *tap*, *tap*, *tap* of typewriter keys late at night where Dr. Warren used to work. There are reports of a transparent couple strolling through the gardens, which many believe is the late doctor and his green-thumbed wife.

Ghost tours love the Old Town Manor and attempt to provoke spirits into uttering EVPs. Ghosts are not confined to Dr. Warren's office (now the Garden Room) or to the gardens. Room 5 is supposed to be particularly haunted. A guest wrote on the Old Town Manor's Facebook page that they awoke in the middle of the night "to find a woman looking out the large window to the right of their bed. When they turned the bedside lamp on, she had vanished."

It could have been Genevieve. Across the street is St. Paul's Episcopal Church. In the church is a large stained-glass window titled *Christ Among the Doctors*. It is dedicated to the Allen and Warren families. Genevieve and William are buried in the Key West Cemetery.

History

Old Town is found on the west side of the island, and it is part of Key West's historic district. Built in 1886, the three-story home in Old Town was originally called Eaton Lodge. Then it was sold to Genevieve's parents, who gifted it to the happy couple. The house had fourteen rooms, cypress doors, pine floors, and ten-foot-high ceilings. The Warrens modified the house in 1937, and the manor includes a fireplace, a wooden bookshelf built into the wall, and an imposing staircase. There used to be a dry goods store near the house, which is now a garage. Another noteworthy feature is the cistern, which Genevieve depended on to water her plants. It is thirty feet high and the tallest water tank in Key West.

Today, Genevieve's garden is still one of the loveliest in Key West, complete with fountains, her prized palm trees, orchids, and valuable and unique trees from foreign lands. In later years, the property was a boardinghouse and, finally, a bed-and-breakfast. It now resides on the National Register of Historic Places.

Address:
Old Town Manor
511 Eaton Street, Key West
305 292 2170

....

CASA GATO/MERCEDES HOSPITAL

Whose spirit is this? we said, because we knew
It was the spirit that we sought and knew.
—Wallace Stevens

"It was been much trouble," she admitted, "and many, many tears."
—Matron Maria Valdez de Gutsens

Ghost Story

Under a black-and-white picture of the former home of Eduardo Gato, there is an accompanying note from Florida Memory (a digital program providing free online access to archival records). It says: "The building is now a guest house and is one of the known 'haunted' buildings in Key West."

It is telling that a state-owned database confirms paranormal activity in an old wooden structure that's been moved at least once from Duval Street to Virginia Street. But there are quite a few credible ghost stories about the Mercedes Hospital.

Exterior of the Old Mercedes Hospital.

Many old hospitals have reputed hauntings. Paranormal investigators at the Historic Sacred Heart Hospital (now a pizza place) in Pensacola reported unintelligible recorded EVPs and strange sounds of claps and crashes. The Spanish Military Hospital in St. Augustine has a lot of paranormal activity, particularly in the back room where soldiers whose wounds were inoperable went to die.

The ghost of Mercedes Hospital appears to be Matron Maria Valdez de Gutsens, who opened the house of healing and worked tirelessly to fund it. She was not a doctor or a nurse: She was an administrator, although she interacted often with patients. She did this for over two decades. Later, the building was divided into apartments, and there are many stories of eerie events involving the late fundraiser.

Residents complained of a woman in old-fashioned garb taking their pulses or their temperature in the middle of the night and vanishing when they sat up. Other residents discussed feeling a presence as though they were not alone in the room. Another resident saw a man and a woman discussing her health as the woman held her wrist. The phantom has also placed a cold hand on sleepers' foreheads. All these incidents ended with the specter fading away into thin air.

All the aforementioned experiences have explanations. Someone who is dreaming wakes up, sits up, and the specter vanishes. And who has not experienced the feeling of being watched by an unknown presence? In actuality, it is a phenomenon scientists call scopaesthesia, which dates back to antiquity but is in no way psychic.

However, the oddest paranormal story about the hospital, which is somewhat believable, concerns a man dying of pneumonia who needed help writing a last letter to his wife and children. But no hospital staff could be spared. The man was in despair.

Miraculously, an older woman showed up, sat beside him, and wrote the letter for the dying man. Later, the patient inquired who the woman might be. He was told in no uncertain terms by hospital staff that only a night nurse was on duty, and she insisted she did not write the letter. Apparently, the man had not yet posted the letter, and it was determined that the handwriting was that of—guess who?—the late Maria Valdez de Gutsens. The actual letter would be evidence of this, because it was presumably dated after her death. But no such evidence exists.

Nonetheless, there is no question Gutsens made the funding and the maintenance of the hospital her life's work, which endured from 1911 until her death in 1941. Although she was buried in the Key West Cemetery, Gutsens's heart and her ghostly presence may still be with the Mercedes Hospital.

History

Originally found on Duval Street, the Gato House was built by an asylum seeker from a foreign government who came to Key West after the Cuban revolution. Eduardo Gato was interested in Cuban politics and nationalism his entire life. He remained in Key West for many years and became immensely wealthy and influential.

It was the Gilded Age in Key West, and Eduardo H. Gato made a lot of money in the cigar business partly because of his connections in Cuba, where all his tobacco came from. Millions of his cigars were sold nationally. As a political patriot of Cuba, he gave away a lot of that money to revolutionary leaders, including José Martí, a freedom fighter known as the father of Cuban independence.

Gato built his wooden Victorian-style home near the ocean as though anticipating a quick getaway. Providing work for carpenters from Cuba, he had them include a walled Spanish-style piazza. But by 1911, Gato no longer lived there. A local Cuban charity, Beneficencia Cubana, prevailed on Gato to lease his house as a hospital for the poor. Ever the generous donor, he agreed to give it to the organizers for free. Gato's only requirement was that they name the hospital after his wife, Mercedes. The hospital was named Casa de la Pobre Mercedes Hospital.

This was where Maria Valdez de Gutsens and other volunteers stepped in to donate their time and money to the less fortunate. This continued until Gutsens's death in 1941. The hospital foundered without her and shut down a year later. The house became known as a way station for squatters and illegal cockfights, which were held in the building's walled Spanish yard. Eventually, the estate was divided up and restored as private residential housing with a historical marker outside. In 1919, Gato sold the property to the City of Key West. The house was moved to 1209 Virginia Street, and today it functions as a guesthouse.

The Gato House/Mercedes Hospital is on the National Register of Historic Places. Both Eduardo Gato and Maria Gutsens are profiled in busts of bronze in the Key West Sculpture Garden.

Address:
Eduardo H. Gato House/Old Mercedes Hospital
1209 Virginia Street, Key West

....

SHOTS AND GIGGLES BAR

Baby, it's hard to shoot a moving target.
—Tennessee Williams

Ghost Story

Shots and Giggles is a dive bar, a sports bar, a bar faithfully attended by locals since 2011. Patrons like to drink beer and watch sports on TV. Tourists come around but not as often and not in droves, like at, say, Sloppy Joe's. But despite its gritty appearance, Shots and Giggles is a laid-back place where you can hang out and afford a few drinks without taking out a loan.

The Shots and Giggles neighborhood bar.

The ghost that haunts this tapered bar is named Frank Fontis, a flamboyant extrovert who was quite a man about town when he was alive. He was pals with Lillian Carter, Jimmy Carter's mother, and chatted with her on her private number. His landscaping work was mentioned in the *Key West Citizen*. Fontis was also widely known as Tennessee Williams's friend, gardener, and handyman; he built the fence that still surrounds the Williams house on Duncan Street. However, tragedy was afoot, and most of it played out in what is now a bar next to a tattoo parlor—in other words, in the very same building where people drunkenly cheer on sports teams: Shots and Giggles.

It happened this way: At some point, Fontis bought the building on the corner of Greene and Ann Streets and called it the Old Coffee Mill and American Railroad Museum. People have strange obsessions, and in Florida, for some reason, grown men playing with trains, talking about trains, and collecting train paraphernalia is common. Fontis was no exception.

Unfortunately, on the night of January 5, 1979, when a naked Frank opened the door of his museum and living quarters, someone shot him point-blank in the head. He died right then and there on his porch. Well, he didn't die right then. By the time someone found him, the forty-nine-year-old had bled out, which meant he was alive for a little while after he was shot. Otherwise, there would not have been as much blood—and there was a veritable pool of it. Bloodstained paper money was scattered around his corpse. Fontis's death seemed like a casualty of the '70s, a violent decade that descended from peace and love into drugs, crime, and rage.

Some money and jewelry were stolen. Later that same night, someone looted Tennessee Williams's home as well. Fortunately, the playwright was in New York and not at home. Williams had been attacked in the streets of Key West, and anti-gay sentiment was presumed to be behind it.

Two drifters were eventually questioned about the Fontis murder, but they were released for lack of evidence. Frank was known to solicit destitute young male "snowbirds," so it is not unlikely that one of them killed him. Robbery was the suspected motive, but the bloodstained money scattered around Fontis's corpse indicate an unorganized, impulsive murder. But no one was ever tried or convicted.

When the police searched the museum, they found items that belonged to Tennessee Williams, items such as an original manuscript. The playwright was incensed to find a friend and an employee had stolen from him. Thereafter, he had nothing good to say about Frank Fontis, calling him a "grotesque man." The Shots and Giggles website goes further, including a Tennessee Williams slur identifying Fontis as a "malign spirit" and claiming he had a "genuine demonic presence…[and] evil powers."

That brings us back to Shots and Giggles. Some people say any press is good press and since Williams has long since gone home to that Sloppy Joe's in the sky, his words contain no actual validity. But it is said that the dead don't like to be forgotten, especially when they are unjustly ejected from life. Frank Fontis is no exception. Glasses fly off the bar, and some seem targeted. There are cold spots and unexplained feelings of dread. Some people walking their dogs cross the street to avoid the bar.

Fontis's murder is like many other homicides in other cities: It's been a cold case for forty-five years, people kind of know who did it, but there is no evidence. It's a topic of speculation, still, in Key West bars, but especially at Shots and Giggles. That is where Frank Fontis died. And it still pisses him off.

HISTORY

The building stood empty until 2011, when owners Steve Kibbe and Hannia Rivera turned it into Shots and Giggles. Given the building's former history, the use of the word *shots* as a double entendre is, if deliberate, stupendously tasteless. But in Key West, maybe not so much, and Hannah and Steve have lived in Key West for decades.

Hannah said she thought up the name of the bar long before she even met her husband and that the name and the building's history are an ironic coincidence. Still, they had a medium come in to try to communicate with whatever spirits were fond of spending eternity in the bar. It could have been the slain Frank Fontis, who reportedly said via EVP, "I'm the one who's been drinking all the rum."

There was no rum missing. Regardless, the couple often plays Fontis's favorite song, "Dancing Queen," which apparently cuts back on the paranormal activity. Steve has speculated that Fontis may enjoy listening to the conversations and gossip in the neighborhood bar.

Erected in 1928, the building is listed as a nightclub on property records and measures just under two thousand square feet. It has a long, dark, narrow bar with a big-screen TV in the corner always playing sports games or horse races. Motorcycles hang from beams in the ceiling. There is a vague mermaid theme to the place, and it is a registered dive bar, which basically means it's inexpensive and no-frills.

Hannah said that the place wasn't even a bar when they bought it. The couple gave the building a thorough renovation in 2011 and added a brick patio in 2012. It's perhaps the only bar in the United States with Davidson on tap. Their signature drink is "Mermaid Water," made from vodka and watermelon lemonade. Apparently, they've given their appearance, marketing, and neighborhood appeal a lot of thought. "Dogs are welcome here," Steve has said. "Ghosts are welcome here."

Patrons pedal there on bicycles in the balmy Key West weather. "Our success here," Hannah says, "depends on relationships"—including with one fractious ghost.

ADDRESS:
SHOTS AND GIGGLES
201 ANN STREET, KEY WEST
305 304 8562

. . . .

THE KAPOK TREES

In the shade of a giving tree, one finds solace and peace.
—Shel Silverstein

Ghost Story

On the southernmost island in the Caribbean, there is a legend about a kapok tree called the Castle of the Devil. According to tradition, every kapok houses resident spirits, either good or evil. In Trinidad, a spirit named Bazil was the soul of one kapok tree. In Greek, *bazil* means "kingly" or "royal." In popular culture, Bazil was used as the name of a tracker for the Jedi Order. Yet according to legend, Bazil, who lived in this particular kapok tree, was neither royal nor an ally. He was a prisoner, tricked into the tree by a human whose soul he coveted. If the tree is ever cut down, Bazil will be free to walk the earth again.

That brings us to the present. There are a limited number of Indonesian kapok trees in Florida. They are mostly found in Palm Beach, Clewiston, Clearwater, St. Petersburg—and Key West. Kapok wood has been used for canoes, tools, furniture, and doors, yet cutting down any kapok tree is said to free the spirits who dwell in the roots and branches. Since kapok trees have a lifespan of well over a century, you have to wonder how many and whose spirits will be released when one falls. With branches akimbo and tree roots as big as a strong man's arm reaching deep into the earth, the trees do resemble legendary gods. People once worshipped them as a symbol of spirituality.

The Mayan dead reputedly climbed the kapok, as their mythological conception of heaven, earth, and hell correlated with the levels of the tree. The Mayan kapok was a sacred tree and marked the center of the universe. All kapok trees are wonders of the world.

History

Found in front of the old Monroe County Court House is a 120-plus-year-old kapok tree, a marvel that most people walk past without a second glance. Small wonder: This is a tree with a website that doesn't work and twenty-nine reviews written by Tripadvisor members, who confirm that, yes, there is an old tree near the Duval Loop bus stop. It is a weird tree, these busy

The rare and mysterious kapok tree.

Key West chickens feed around the roots of the kapok tree.

advisors write, a beautiful tree, but a tree nevertheless, fit for the background of some photo op.

The kapok tree is much more than a place to pose for a selfie. Found in South American rainforests, the kapok is rare in Florida, and it matures only in southern Florida. Kapok trees grow fast and grow to enormous heights, up to thirteen feet per year. In the wild, they can live to be eight hundred years old. The tree houses numerous species of wildlife, and Key West chickens peck near the roots of the kapok, shaded from broiling summer rays by the tree's enormous boughs.

Also known as the silk-cotton tree, the kapok has palm-shaped leaves. Its flowers, grouped in buds of three to six, have an odor repellent to humans but seductive to some species of bats who pollinate the tree. The kapok grows pointy thorns and has an oblong seed pouch of soft, thready down. During World War II, the kapok pod fiber, weightless and resistant to water, was used to make life jackets for soldiers. In fact, it is still used in the manufacture of life jackets and buoys.

The kapok tree is a Key West Historical Landmark. There are three other kapok trees located in front of the Harvey Government Center on Truman Avenue. These trees were planted in 1915.

Address:
The old kapok tree in front of
the old Monroe County Court House
502 Whitehead Street, Key West

....

CAPTAIN GEORGE CAREY'S HOUSE

The land was ours before we were the land's.
—Robert Frost

Ghost Story

Captain George Carey's house has a history dating back long before the Englishman was born. Key West was mostly unsettled in the eighteenth

Captain George Carey's house and the Pirates Well.

century, but people did come ashore—whether they were pirates, explorers, or refugees—and they typically came for the water. It is said even Ponce de León was not really looking for the Fountain of Youth as much as he was looking for potable water to take back to his ship. He would have been happy, two centuries later, to amble across 410 Caroline Street. There is a sign displayed in the front of the house that says: "First fresh water found on island and used by pirates in the 1700s."

The Pirates Well was not the only water source. Fresh water arrived sometimes by boat and, later, via Henry Flagler's train; much later, it was hauled in over the highway. Today there is a water pipeline that runs from Florida City to Key West with stations along the way to maintain pressure, which at times is notoriously low throughout the Keys. The main water pipeline is half a century old, and although repairs are handled with the Florida Aqueduct Authority, nothing is going to change soon about the groundwater supply of moderately hard water that trickles from Keys showers.

However insufficient Keys residents find the local water supply in the present day, it is nothing compared to how the people of the eighteenth century coped. A primary source of water was tabby-concrete cisterns, which caught and stored the rain. Yet in the early days of Keys colonization, there was a place in the center of historic Key West: a well of seemingly inexhaustible fresh water. Pirates knew about it and paid local merchants for the water. Perhaps the payment was to ensure their silence.

Everyone knows pirates were the first anarchists, each his own man or woman, beholden to no one. They were also violent, lawless, and armed. So it is no surprise to learn that the Pirates Well was a site of betrayal and vengeance, where the best man won and the loser went down the well—or so the legend goes. It is hard to believe that no one noticed the tainted water, if the legend was true. But local citizens swear that on summer nights, passersby sometimes hear whispers around or in the well. It's supposed to be especially eerie in the dark, when the well sometimes casts a green aura.

There are stories of buried treasure all over Florida, on land as well as at sea. Could the whispers of the well reveal secrets to such booty? The Pirates Well is rumored to be the site of buried treasure as well as decomposing pirates. One of the owners reported finding a complete skeleton on the grounds. This was a common practice among pirates: the abettor ending up guarding the swag from the bottom up.

HISTORY

The Pirates Well has thirteen reviews written by Tripadvisor members who are singularly unimpressed with it and its history except as a photo op. It's only a freshwater well from the 1700s used by pirates and located at the site of the second-oldest home in Key West; take a picture and move on.

The site was significantly more important to the local pirates and merchants who used the well for fresh water. By the nineteenth century, there was an original owner of the house: Captain George Carey, an Englishman, a descendant of William the Conqueror (according to Carey), and a Key West settler. He built the wooden house in 1834, which today is the second-oldest house in Key West. Carey made a lot of money selling wholesale liquor to retail merchants. He was a man about town—at least until he met his wife, a German woman aboard a ship that was wrecked. Carey saved her life and then married her. The house was originally only two rooms and a separate cookhouse; in 1844, he renovated the house to accommodate his bride.

Located at 410 Caroline Street, the snug wooden structure is built in the Classic Revival Conch architectural style. Such houses are typically rectangular wooden homes with gables and a columned porch extending the width of the house.

In addition to Captain George Carey, another illustrious owner of the house was Jesse Porter, a native Conch and a historical preservationist who saved many of Key West's old homes and buildings. She renovated the Caroline Street house, adding floors, doors, and porches. The home on Caroline Street was the portal for many celebrities of the day to see and to be seen.

On the right side of the house is a smaller cottage where Vermont Nobel laureate poet Robert Frost stayed as a winter guest of Miss Porter's. It was there he wrote many of his famous poems, including "The Gift Outright," which he read at John F. Kennedy's first inauguration.

After Jesse Porter died, the house was a museum for a while, but it was eventually sold to a private owner. The Pirates Well is part of the Historic Key West walking tour, and it is a Historic Key West Landmark.

Address:
Captain George Carey's House
410 Caroline Street, Key West

....

SHEL SILVERSTEIN'S HOUSE

Let us leave this place where the smoke blows black
and the dark street winds and bends.
—Shel Silverstein

Ghost Story

This ghost story is about banyan trees in front of Shel Silverstein's house. The trees' influence was both prophetic and practical concerning the famous author's work.

Related to the strangler fig, banyan trees look like huge roots, which they are, although the roots become trunks eventually. People who plant banyan

Shel Silverstein's former home.

trees aren't usually aware of their propensity to swallow objects whole. It sounds crazy, but it's true. With its system of airborne roots, a huge banyan tree in Taiwan swallowed a warehouse. It took seventy years, but we're talking significant square footage.

It took only a few months for the banyan tree to swallow the bicycle in front of Shel Silverstein's house. The writer left his bike leaning against the tree and went away for a while; when he returned, the tree had wound its roots around the bicycle, literally lifting it off the ground and incorporating it into its mass until it could no longer be seen. Anyone familiar with Silverstein's children's book *The Giving Tree* cannot miss the irony of an apparent "taking" tree right in the author's yard.

Silverstein died in the house on Williams Street of a heart attack on May 10, 1999. And there are no stories of him haunting his former home.

However, legend has it that the banyan tree incorporates spirits of the living who reside in its roots. People cross the street rather than pass a banyan tree in the dark.

In 2017, winds from Hurricane Irma destroyed Silverstein's wooden home, sending the two banyan trees crashing through the interior front of the house. The storm also visibly tore up the sidewalk in jagged concrete chunks, reminiscent of the Silverstein book of poems *Where the Sidewalk Ends*, which the poet wrote in memory of his daughter. The hurricane made his former home a total loss; it was condemned, and there was little to be done except tear it down.

After the hurricane propelled massive banyan trees like missiles toward Silverstein's Key West home, some people speculated that it was almost as if nature was venting its frustration over Silverstein's *The Giving Tree*, in which an unnamed, once-majestic tree is reduced to a stump and declares itself happy.

Fortunately, a local company, Kanga Construction, took the former Greek Revival house on as a historic preservation project. Kanga created a carbon copy of Shel Silverstein's house the way it was before the hurricane. Then it replanted the two banyan trees in the front yard, hoping they would live. As of this writing, they are alive and border the edges of Silverstein's former property.

Let's just hope another hurricane doesn't rile the spirit of the banyan trees up and into the house again.

History

Shel Silverstein grew up in Chicago but lived quietly for many years in the Key West house with the columns and pilasters. He mostly lived alone, and there are conflicting stories about whether he was ever married. The famous artist and author of children's literature actually had two children of his own. He was the father to a daughter, Shoshanna Hastings, who died at eleven years of age from a cerebral aneurysm, and a son named Matthew DeVer, who became a singer, songwriter, and producer. However, after Silverstein's death, his sister applied for control of his estate, and it is unlikely she would have received it if the famous writer had a wife, even an ex-wife.

Silverstein is best known for his quirky, somewhat dark children's poetry and stories; it is not widely recognized that he was a songwriter as well, penning such classics as "A Boy Named Sue," "The Cover of the Rolling

Stone," and "Sylvia's Mother." He wrote title tracks for famous movies such as *Postcards from the Edge* and contributed several pieces to Marlo Thomas's signature 1970s work *Free to Be... You and Me*.

Playwright David Mamet claimed in an article for the *Paris Review* that he experienced severe chest pains the same night Sheldon Allan Silverstein died of two massive heart attacks endured hours apart. They were best friends.

Address:
Shel Silverstein's House
618 William Street, Key West

....

KEY WEST HISTORIC MEMORIAL SCULPTURE GARDEN

There are so many vivid, larger-than-life figures
who have been part of this city's past, it's apparently hard
for the selection committee to choose among them.
—Joy Williams

Ghost Story

The ghost story about the Key West Historic Memorial Sculpture Garden has to do with the experience of a former employee of a local restaurant. Let's call him Peter.

Peter was enjoying a smoke within the confines of the gated sculpture garden. It was close to eight o'clock in the evening, and everything was shutting down. The gates to the sculpture garden would be locked soon. In the gathering twilight, the expressive bronze busts of the eminent men and women of Key West seemed to follow Peter with their eyes. Then a man in a felt hat and a windbreaker, far too substantial for the tropical twilight, entered the garden, keeping his back to the young man.

Peter hurriedly puffed on his cigarette. It was almost closing time, and he had work to do. In the dusk, the stranger looked like Peter's boss. "Hey," he called. The stranger stood before the bronze busts. He didn't turn around. Peter thought that was weird.

"Hey," he said again. He walked up to the man and, without meaning to, blew a stream of cigarette smoke in his face. The smoke drifted through the man's image as though it were air. Peter stepped back and looked into the man's face. The eyes were piercing in the gathering darkness, sort of like the eyes of the assembled busts. And then the apparition disappeared.

"It was the weirdest thing," Peter recalled. "I'd never had an interaction with something on a different plane. But I'm a believer now."

This happened in 2016, the year the artist and sculptor James Mastin died.

History

The garden is located in Old Town on the island's original shoreline, which is located adjacent to Mallory Square. It is now the Key West Historic Memorial Sculpture Garden, which opened in 1997. A large bronze statue called *The Wreckers* dominates the space, featuring two burly men salvaging cargo and saving a little girl.

The sculpture garden also contains thirty-nine bronze busts of notable Key West movers and shakers. Henry Flagler of Palm Beach is included because of his contributions to the Overseas Railroad. The busts and the *Wreckers* statue were created by American sculptor James Mastin. In 1987, he created a memorial sculpture garden in the Bahamas featuring twenty-nine notable Bahamian citizens and a large bronze sculpture called *The Landing*.

The Key West Sculpture Garden's bust of Hemingway.

There is room in the Key West garden for an additional thirty-one busts, but one hasn't been added since famed playwright and Key Wester Tennessee Williams was included in 2018. It was Mastin's last bronze bust, exhibited posthumously. He died in 2016 in Miami.

The assemblance of outdoor art includes former slaves, captains, poets, politicians, a nun, Cuban revolutionaries, wreckers, writers, fishermen, a former president, and more. It is free and funded by private donations raised by the Friends of Mallory Square.

Mastin's wife and children attended the twenty-year celebration of the artist's work in the Key West Sculpture Garden. The garden itself is a National Historic Landmark.

There is a Walkway of History comprised of bricks you can buy and inscribe. It's not cheap, and you get only sixty characters, but the silver lining is that unlike the bronze busts, you can get one while you're still alive.

Address:
Key West Historic Memorial Sculpture Garden
401 Wall Street, Key West
(next to El Meson de Pepe's Restaurant)
305 294 4142

....

FANTASY FEST PARADE

We're still the local authority for all things haunted in Cayo Hueso.
—David Sloane, author and founder of the first Key West Ghost Tour

Things have gone too far.
—Paul Menta, founder of Key West Legal Rum

Ghost Story

In an ironic twist, three years after organizers and the mayor mused about ridding Fantasy Fest of the word *fantasy*, the elected grand marshal of the 2024 event was the notorious Robert the Doll and his appointed doll keeper, David Sloane. Sloane is an author and the owner and founder of the Key West Ghost Hunt, established in the late '90s as the "first ghost tour" in America. It quickly caught on, particularly in a Southern city where there had been a lot of yellow fever deaths and consequent paranormal activity.

Robert the Doll is considerably more famous than Sloane or the doll's original owner, Robert Gene Otto, an accomplished Key West artist. Otto would probably never have gotten an invitation to be grand marshal, despite his talent. Conversely, Robert's fame as a haunted and belligerent doll has

Fantasy Fest in Key West.

spread far and wide. On Amazon alone, there are books, DVDs, and even a TV show based on his malign presence and disposition. He was the role model for the movie *Chucky*.

Robert is also the first object of irrational reverence to lead the Fantasy Fest parade. Past grand marshals were human performers, including Kool & the Gang, Dolly Parton, David Schwimmer, Kelly Clarkson, Styx, Lionel Richie, Sting, and Jimmy Buffett.

There are no reports of Robert creating mischief as grand marshal. Although it is commonly believed that pictures can't be taken of Robert without his permission or dire consequences ensue, David Sloane affirms that Robert metes out punishment only for direct disrespect, such as people giving him the finger or sticking out their tongues. Certainly, the sixty thousand people who took pictures of Robert the Doll at the 2024 Fantasy Fest Parade weren't cursed.

Or were they?

If you attended Fantasy Fest 2024, took pictures of Robert the Doll, and experienced a string of bad luck (kitchen mishaps, falls, flat tires, and so on), you just may wish to write Robert a letter of apology, care of the East Martello Museum.

HISTORY

On October 26, 2024, the Key West Fantasy Fest Parade on Duval Street celebrated its forty-fifth year with the theme "It's a '90s neon cosmic carnival." Although there is still nudity, giant ghouls and skeletons, costume parties, marches, and lots and lots of recyclable beads—reminiscent of Mardi Gras—city officials have not formally made the parade "family friendly" by slapping decency law misdemeanors on unclothed participants. They've thought about it, though.

Any time large crowds of drunken people get together, there is bound to be controversy. Events for children take place the last Sunday of the festival, but no one in his right mind would take a child to the main Fantasy Fest parade (officially called the Deep Eddy Vodka Fantasy Fest Parade) that marches through Duval Street on the last Saturday night of the festival. This is the night everyone lets it all hang out, literally, and flaunts their lack of decorum for all to see, in the streets and on large motorized floats. The participant groups are called krewes, just like folks at Mardi Gras parades.

The idea of the parade started in the 1970s, during a downturn in tourism. At that time, the Keys were famous more for square groupers than an international street party. But local business owners put on their thinking caps about a way to start off the season in October with a rousing bang. They had a sweltering summer behind them, a Halloween holiday in their favor, and a city prone to flamboyant themes and costumes. The first Fantasy Fest Parade was in 1979, and hardly anyone went. But everyone heard about it.

Fantasy Fest Parade hasn't missed a year since—except in 2005, when it was held in December because of Hurricane Wilma, and in 2020, when it was canceled because of COVID-19. Forty-five years after its inception, Fantasy Fest is still going strong during the last week in October. In addition, some events raise funds for local nonprofits.

Key West participants decorate businesses and houses with the year's current theme, just like New Orleans. Winners in categories such as Best Overall in Entertainment, Costume, Theme, Walking Group, and Conch Style receive cash prizes and notoriety. Jaimie Gwidt's Key West Kreatives won first prize of $6,000 in 2024 for their "Flagler's 1890 Fantasy Float," complete with train and costumed attendants.

The theme for the 2025 Fantasy Fest Parade: "Bedtime Stories and Magical Monsters."

Address:
Key West Fantasy Fest
Duval Street, Key West

....

The Basilica of Saint Mary Star of the Sea

As long as the grotto stands,
Key West will never experience the full brunt of a hurricane.
—Sister Louis Gabriel

Ghost Story

This is not exactly a ghost story. It is more like a miracle.

On September 8, 1919, there was a terrible hurricane in Key West with 110-mile-per-hour winds. Several hundred people died. The city of Key West and a church, Saint Mary Star of the Sea, experienced acute destruction. It was the third such hurricane Sister Louis Gabriel experienced since her tenure with the Sisters of the Holy Names of Jesus and Mary, beginning in 1897. She had borne enough of the devastation nature wrought on the innocent. Sister Gabriel determined she would appeal to the Holy Mother for help.

Sister Gabriel was no stranger to hardship, sickness, or work. In 1898, during the Spanish-American War, she nursed soldiers, and during the yellow fever epidemic, she contracted the disease herself and undertook a long convalescence.

Grotto at the Basilica of Saint Mary Star of the Sea.

For the nun, the salvation of the tiny island beleaguered by behemoth storms was to design a grotto fashioned after the famous site discovered by Bernadette Soubirous in Lourdes in 1858. Bernadette claimed apparitions of the mother of Christ appeared to her in the small French cave on three separate occasions. A spring of water was discovered nearby, and evidence of miracles from those who bathed in or drank from it appears in ecclesiastical records. Mindful of the healing power of Lourdes, Sister Gabriel raised funds and re-created the Lourdes grotto on church grounds a little south of the Saint Mary Star of the Sea church.

The grotto, made from Key West rocks, was dedicated on the Feast of the Ascension, May 25, 1922, to Our Lady of Lourdes and to Saint Bernadette. Sister Gabriel predicted that its presence would protect the southernmost island, and that "Key West would never again experience the full brunt of a hurricane."

Sister Gabriel died on September 13, 1948. Three weeks later, a hurricane stormed the island to minimal effect. Key West Conchs claim there has not been a severe hurricane on the island since the creation of the grotto, which is often in the news when a hurricane approaches the Keys. The National Weather Service bureau in Key West is not consulted nearly as often.

Interior of the church and the stained-glass depiction of the Blessed Mother.

Hurricane George made landfall in Key West in 1998, causing destruction of property, flooding, and power outages. It was a category 2 storm with 105-mile-per-hour winds. People in Alabama died during this hurricane, but no lives were lost in the Keys. Hurricane Irma also stormed Key West in 2017, but the worst of the damage occurred in the middle Keys. No one in Key West died.

Perhaps Sister Gabriel's grotto is not eliminating hurricanes but instead tempering their full force.

History

The Basilica of Saint Mary Star of the Sea, like most churches in Florida, was originally a wooden church in a different location. It burned down; its website hints at an arsonist. The present Saint Mary Star of the Sea Church on Windsor Lane went up in 1904. The church is made of poured concrete from limestone dug from the church soil; the architecture is American Victorian with Gothic arches and stained glass. Ernest Hemingway donated an altar to the church after attending services with his Catholic wife, Pauline.

Dedicated and blessed in 1907, the stained-glass window above the altar in Saint Mary Star of the Sea is illuminated by sunlight during the day. A star crowns a young Mary and her child as a ship wrecks on a reef in the background, and a lighthouse is silhouetted by waves and a fiery sunset. Its star is a signal of hope in a time of sorrow.

The Basilica of St. Mary Star of the Sea is one of the oldest Catholic parishes in the state of Florida. Mass services are held in English, Spanish, and Haitian Creole. The church is a part of the Key West Historic District and is on the National Register of Historic Places.

Address:
Historic Grotto
1010 Windsor Lane, Key West
305 294 1018

. . . .

THE DRY TORTUGAS: JEFFERSON KEY

I never saw either of the parties before,
nor can I conceive who sent them to my house.
—Samuel A. Mudd

GHOST STORY

One cannot address ghost stories at Fort Jefferson without first acknowledging its most famous prisoner. That would be Dr. Samuel Mudd, the man who inspired the derisive phrase "Your name is mud." Mudd was a liar, and he deserved to go to prison.

History has been kind to him, alleging that he set the leg of Lincoln's assassin because he didn't know who he was and that he was just fulfilling his Hippocratic oath. In truth, Mudd and Booth met on at least four other documented occasions. Mudd was a Confederate, and he knew what he was doing by not turning Booth over to the authorities. He could have saved himself from prison at Fort Jefferson in the Dry Tortugas. He could have done the right thing.

But Mudd did not do the right thing. He gave the murderer of a president shelter, and he lied about it. Supposedly he redeemed himself by tending to

Floor of the inlet at the Dry Tortugas. *Photo by Cassidy M. Jasmann.*

Fort Jefferson on Garden Key.

yellow fever victims at the remote fort. After four years of imprisonment (he was sentenced to life), he was pardoned by President Andrew Johnson, an avowed former Confederate. Lincoln had switched from Maine's Hannibal Hamlin to Tennessee's Andrew Johnson as vice president for his second term in an effort to woo Southern votes. Instead, Johnson pardoned an accomplice to Lincoln's murder.

But first, Mudd served four years in a virtual hell on earth. It was not called the Dry Tortugas for nothing. Potable water had to be shipped in. It was hot, full of mosquitos and spoiled food, and too far away for visitors. Mudd was reviled for his role in Lincoln's assassination. His accomplices were hanged.

So what does that tell us of the ghosts of Fort Jefferson? For one thing, haunted places often go hand in hand with a geographic history of despair, disease, and betrayal. Yellow fever victims who died there are said to haunt the eerie passageways with moans, shrieks, and death rattles. Specters of Civil War soldiers still stand guard. And Mudd's spirit is said to drift through purgatory and the walls of the old infirmary, tending to soldiers stricken with yellow fever—for eternity.

History

There are seven Keys (Garden, Loggerhead, Bush, Long, East, Hospital, and Middle) jointly known as the Dry Tortugas. Seventy miles west of Key

West, in the Gulf of Mexico, is the island of Garden Key, and the site of Dry Tortugas National Park. Ponce de León visited in 1524, looking for water (potable water, not the Fountain of Youth).

The site of the isolated, unfinished Fort Jefferson on Garden Key served first as a site of a lighthouse, then as a lookout for soldiers to detect pirates and enemies on the Florida Strait, and finally as a military fortress. American commodores feared a hostile takeover of Key West, which Fort Jefferson prevented. The fort also aided in the housing of Union soldiers during the Civil War, effectively blocking shipments of Southern goods. Thousands of soldiers were stationed on the island in the mid-1860s.

Construction of the fort, named after Thomas Jefferson, began during Polk's term as president in 1846, and he never lived to see it—or the Key West fort that bears his name. It took real effort to erect the fort in the fragile ecosystem. Sixteen million bricks were shipped from the North, and it was a long haul to the Dry Tortugas.

The fort was never finished despite almost twenty years of hard labor under a broiling sun, mostly done by slaves. The military feared that extra weight from cannons and bricks could cause the island to destabilize. Nevertheless, Fort Jefferson is the largest brick structure in the United States.

Gun rooms, towers, spiral staircases, and cannons are well preserved at Fort Jefferson, now a tourist spot. There is a beautiful reef bordered by a white sandy beach. Snorkelers swim with angelfish and observe barracudas, nurse sharks, and sea turtles. The sooty tern returns yearly to nest.

There used to be a pontoon plane service to the island. The only way to get there now is by boat. If you don't have a friend who can sail the Gulf of Mexico, there are two ferries that leave daily from Key West. It's a two-hour trip and can cost a couple hundred dollars or more—which is a bargain, considering.

The island bears witness to Florida history and to American history. Despite the long-ago imprisonment of an American traitor, the beautiful island's reputation is in no way stuck in the Mudd.

Fort Jefferson is a national monument.

Address:
Dry Tortugas National Park
68 miles west of Key West in the Gulf of Mexico

....

BIBLIOGRAPHY

Abaco Sun. "Key West Memorial Sculpture Garden Honours James Mastin." January 8, 2018. https://abacosun.com.

Adelson, Fred. "Remembering Seward Johnson, Founder of Grounds for Sculpture." *New Jersey Courier-Post*, March 19, 2020.

Amberg, Marion. *Mary's Miracles: A Traveler's Guide to Catholic America*. Our Sunday Visitor, 2022.

Audubon House & Tropical Gardens. "Meet Our Ghosts." https://audubonhouse.org.

Bak, John S. *Tennessee Williams: A Literary Life*. Palgrave Macmillan, 2013.

Baraniak, Justyna, and Malgorzata Kania-Dobrowolska. "Multi-Purpose Utilization of Kapok Fiber and Properties of *Ceiba Pentandra* Tree in Various Branches of Industry." *Journal of Natural Fibers* 20, no. 1 (2023). https://doi.org/10.1080/15440478.2023.2192542.

Basilica of St. Mary Star of the Sea. https://stmarykeywest.com.

Bender & Associates Architects. *Monroe County Historic Jail*. Historic Structure Report, prepared for Monroe County Board of County Commissioners, January 2018.

Bertelli, Brad. "Keys History: Arrival of Fresh Water Brought Relief to Island Chain." *Keys Weekly*, June 6, 2023.

———. "Keys History: Fishing Lodges, Brothels & the No Name Pub." *Keys Weekly*, August 29, 2022.

———. "Keys History: Florida Keys' Bahia Honda Island Bustled with Activity." *Keys Weekly*, July 1, 2022.

———. "Keys History: Isaac Allerton Wreck Off Key West Had Valuable Goods to Salvage." *Keys Weekly*, May 26, 2023.

———. "Keys History: John Geiger Goes from Wrecker to Wealthy Man." *Keys Weekly*, March 16, 2022.

———. "Keys History: No Name Key Property Had Trees & Traps." *Keys Weekly*, August 12, 2022.

———. "Keys History: The Origins of Alabama Jacks." *Keys Weekly*, October 18, 2024.

Bertelli, Brad, and Jerry Wilkinson. *Islamorada*. Arcadia Publishing, 2014.

Blackerby, Cheryl. "Flagler-Built Casa Marina Has Rich Past, Magical Moments." *Palm Beach Daily News*, September 24, 2016.

Blais, Madeleine. "Tennessee in the Tropics." *Washington Post*, April 3, 1979.

Blevin, Kip. "Museum Holds Wrecker's Lure." *Key West Citizen*, July 28, 1989.

Blinckmann, Hays. "Shel Silverstein's House Destroyed." *Keys Weekly*, September 28. 2017.

Blitz, Matt. "The True Story of Ernest Hemingway's Favorite Bar." *Food and Wine*, June 22, 2017.

Brown, Alan. *Ghosts of Florida's Gulf Coast*. Globe Pequot, 2015.

———. *Haunted Places in the American South*. University Press of Mississippi, 2002.

Browne, Jefferson Beale. *Key West, the Old and the New*. Record Company, 1912.

Burke, J. Wills. *The Streets of Key West: A History Through Street Names*. Pineapple Press, 2004.

Burns, Ken, and Lynn Novik. *Hemingway*. Six-part documentary, PBS, April 2021.

Callaway, Linda. "Iguana: Symbolism, Meanings, and History." Symbol Genie, October 25, 2022. https://symbolgenie.com.

Captain Tony's Saloon. "Saloon History." http://www.capttonyssaloon.com.

Carlisle, Rodney. *Key West in History*. Pineapple Press, 2015.

Casa Marina Resort Key West. https://casamarinaresort.com.

Cherry, Lynne. *The Great Kapok Tree: A Tale of the Amazon Rain Forest*. Harcourt Brace Jovanovich, 1990.

Conway, John. "African Cemetery at Higgs Beach, Key West, Florida." Atlas Obscura, January 7, 2019. https://www.atlasobscura.com.

Desmarais, Cricket. "Meet Alex Vega: Retired Fire Captain Fans Flames of History." *Keys Weekly*, September 22, 2022.

Diddle, Albert W. "Medical Events in the History of Key West." *Tequesta* 6 (1946): 14–37.

Dwork, David. "No 'Quick Fix': Florida Keys Water Pressure to Be Reduced Indefinitely." WPLG Local 10, March 23, 2023.

Filosa, Gwen. "Giant 'Kiss' Lands in Key West." *Florida Keys News*, January 11, 2017.

Find a Grave. "George W. Carey." https://www.findagrave.com.

Fisher, Jerry. *The Pacesetter: The Untold Story of Carl G. Fisher.* Friesen Press, 1998.

Florida Baptist Historical Society. "The Journal of Florida Baptist Heritage." Vol. 25, 2023. https://floridabaptisthistory.org/wp-content/uploads/2023/11/JOURNAL-FINAL-11-1-23.pdf.

Florida Keys News. "Key West's Famed Casa Marina Resort to Celebrate 100 Year Anniversary." January 2, 2021.

Florida Memory. "A Healthful Haunting." 2018. https://www.floridamemory.com.

Frawley-Holler, Janis. *Key West Gardens and Their Stories*. Pineapple Press, 2000.

Genn, Island. "Key West Famous Resident Profile: Tennessee Williams." Key Wester, March 3, 2022. https://thekeywester.com.

———. "Key West: Higgs Beach." Key Wester, March 16, 2012. https://thekeywester.com.

———. "The Key West Sculpture Garden: Where History Meets Art." Key Wester, December 31, 2024. https://thekeywester.com.

Ghost City Tours. "Ghosts of Hemingway's House." https://ghostcitytours.com.

Ghosts and Gravestones of Key West. "Haunted Guide to Captain Tony's Saloon." Accessed August 28, 2024. https://www.ghostsandgravestones.com.

Gottlieb, Alma. *Under the Kapok Tree: Identity and Difference in Beng Thought*. University of Chicago Press, 1996.

Gross, Bonnie. "Historic Key West Cemetery: A Scenic Stop That Is Full of Stories." Florida Rambler, July 5, 2024.

Guerry, Jean U. "The Matecumbe Methodist Church." *Tequesta* 30 (1970): 64–68.

Hauck, Dennis. *Haunted Places: The National Directory.* Penguin Books, 2002.

Hepburn, Donald S. "Florida Baptist Church Affiliation with Baptist Associations Between 1821 and the Mid-1850s." *Journal of Florida Baptist Heritage* 25 (2023): 26.

Hill, Catherine. "Measuring Success in the Redevelopment of Former Military Bases: Evidence from a Case Study of the Truman Annex in Key West, Florida." *Economic Development Quarterly* 14, no. 3, 2000: 267–77.

Hingston, Sandy. "12 Things You Might Not Know About John James Audubon." *Philadelphia Magazine*, April 26, 2016.

HistoryNet. "Dr. Samuel A. Mudd: The Man Who Helped J. Wilkes Booth Assassinate Lincoln." November 13, 2019. https://www.historynet.com.

Hobbs, Kevin. "Three Trees That Tell the Story of Ancient Cultures." *Literary Hub*, February 20, 2020. https://lithub.com.

Homan, Lynn M., and Thomas Reilly. *Key West.* Arcadia Publishing, 2000.

Hunt, Bruce. *Visiting Small Town Florida: A Guide to 79 of Florida's Most Interesting Small Towns*. Pineapple Press, 2021.

Huriash, Lisa. "Exhibit Pieces Chronicle Jews' Contributions to Miami Beach." *Tallahassee Democrat*, February 14, 1999.

Jenkins, Greg. *Florida's Ghostly Legends.* Pineapple Press, 2005.

Jukofsky, Diane. *Encyclopedia of Rainforests*. Oryx Press, 2002.

Karras, Alan L. "'Custom Has the Force of Law': Local Officials and Contraband in the Bahamas and the Floridas, 1748–1779." *Florida Historical Quarterly* 80, no. 3 (2002): 281–311. http://www.jstor.org/stable/30149240.

Key West Art & Historical Society. "Henry M. Flagler, Builder of the Overseas Railroad." 2025. https://www.kwahs.org.

———. "Key West Lighthouse & Keeper's Quarters Museum." 2024. https://www.kwahs.org.

Key West Author's Co-op. *Beyond Paradise: More New Fiction from the Florida Keys*. Key West Authors' Co-op, 1999.

Kushlan, James Anthony, and Kirsten Hines. *Dry Tortugas National Park*. Arcadia Publishing, 2019.

Lee, Catherine. "Fantasy Fest Draws Crowd of 35,000." *Key West Citizen*, November 2, 1987.

Lovering, Frank. "Lovering Tells History of Construction of Martello Towers in Island City." *Key West Citizen*, October 19, 1950.

Lynch, Marika. "Sordid History Bites the Dust: Keys Jail Razed." *Miami Herald*, January 11, 1998.

Maloney, Walter C. *A Sketch of the History of Key West*. Advertiser Printing House, 1876.

Mamet, David. "He Was My Closest Friend." *Paris Review*, March 11, 2014.

Matecumbe Historical Trust Corporation. "A Guide to Historic Islamorada." 2022. https://matecumbehistoricaltrust.org/wp-content/uploads/2022/11/MHTbrochure.pdf.

Mathis, Sara. "The Mystery of the Hammerhead." *Keys Weekly*, November 21, 2018.

McEvoy, George. "A Grim Drama in Key West: The Death of Frank Fontis." *Fort Lauderdale News*, May 20, 1979.

McIver, Stuart B. *Hemingway's Key West.* Pineapple Press, 2001.

McIver, Stuart. *Death in the Everglades: The Murder of Guy Bradley, America's First Martyr to Environmentalism.* University Press of Florida, 2009.

Mel Fisher Museum. "African Cemetery at Higgs Beach." 2016. https://www.africanburialgroundathiggsbeach.org.

Miami Herald. "Her Nude Body Was Found 30 Years Ago, Slashed and Heartless. Who Killed Lisa Sanders?" December 26, 2018.

Miles, Mandy. "Key West Ends New Year Parties at 10 P.M.—How'd That Go?" *Keys Weekly*, January 3, 2021.

Mulligan, Hugh. "The Florida Keys: The End of the Rainbow." *Sarasota Herald Tribune*, June 22, 1969.

Murphy, George. *The Key West Reader: The Best of Key West Writers 1830–1990.* Tortugas, 1989.

National Center for Missing and Exploited Children. "Jane Bahia Honda Key Doe 1979." Monroe County Sheriff's Office (Florida) Major Crimes Unit, Homicide. https://www.missingkids.org/poster/NCMU/1115295/1.

National Parks Service. "Dry Tortugas: History & Culture." https://www.nps.gov.

Nolan, David. "The Fort East Martello Museum: a Haunted Destination Not to Be Missed." *Sloan's Haunted Key West* (blog), 2023. https://www.hauntedkeywest.com.

O' Hara, Timothy. "Farewell Fantasy Fest?" *Key West Citizen*, December 11–12, 2021.

Payne, Stefanie, and Jonathan Irish. *A Year in the National Parks: The Greatest American Road Trip*. Fire Soul, n.d.

Playground Daily News. "Ghost of Nurse Haunts Key West House." November 4, 1976.

Powell, Lewis. "Night Nurse on Duty." *Southern Spirit Guide: A Guide to the Ghosts and Hauntings of the American South* (blog), March 20, 2014. https://www.southernspiritguide.org.

Powers, Mathew. "Eduardo H. Gato House." Clio: Your Guide to History, March 8, 2021. https://theclio.com.

PraveenMohan. "The Haunted Club Chameleon—Key West, Florida." YouTube, October 19, 2015. https://youtu.be/jGbTU5d5QME.

Radar, Dotson. "Tennessee Williams: A Friendship." *Paris Review* 81 (Fall 1981).

Reilly, Lucas. "The Most Dangerous Job: The Murder of America's First Bird Warden." Mental Floss, October 2018. https://www.mentalfloss.com.

Richardson, Laura. "Stanley Papio." *Florida Weekly*, May 3, 2018.

Rode, Randy. "Big Mo and the Bruisers: All Out Combat with Sharks Off the Florida Keys." *Sports Illustrated* (September 2008).

Rodewig, Cheryl. "Nearly 300 African Refugees Are Memorialized Outside a Repurposed Civil War Fort in Key West." Roadtrippers, August 2021. https://roadtrippers.com.

San Carlos Institute. "History of the San Carlos Institute." https://www.institutosancarlos.org.

Saunders, Nicolas. *The Encyclopedia of Caribbean Archeology and Traditional Culture.* ABC-CLIO, 2005.

Self, Lynda. "The Ernest Hemingway House and Museum in Key West." Southern Kissed, June 20, 2023. https://www.southernkissed.com.

Shaughnessy, Carol. "Pirates, Wreckers and Treasure Hunters Helped Shape Florida Keys." *Keys Voices*, July 15, 2020.

Silver, Vernon. "Penalver: Money Can Be Raised." *Key West Citizen*, June 18, 1992.

Sloan, David L. *Ghosts of Key West*. Phantom Press, 1998.

———. *Robert the Doll*. Phantom Press, 2014.

Sloan, David. "The Key West Cemetery." *Sloan's Haunted Key West* (blog), 2023. https://www.hauntedkeywest.com.

Sloan's Haunted Key West (blog). "Explore Key West's Haunted Landmarks and Museums!" 2024. https://www.hauntedkeywest.com.

Southernmost Ghosts. "Shots and Giggles: The Bizarre Tale of Frank Fontis." October 15, 2024. https://southernmostghosts.com.

Stalter, Richard. "The Vascular Flora of Garden Key and Fort Jefferson, Dry Tortugas National Park, Florida, U.S.A." *Journal of the Botanical Research Institute of Texas* 10, no. 2 (2016): 527–34. http://www.jstor.org/stable/44858597.

Stansfield, Charles A. *Haunted Presidents: Ghosts in the Lives of the Chief Executives*. Stackpole Books, 2010.

Starling, Marlowe. "Flocks of Flamingos Returned to a Rejuvenated Everglades." *Audubon Magazine* (Fall 2024).

Startt, Kristina. "Skeletal Pathologies Observed Within a Cemetery Sample from Key West." Thesis presented to Florida Gulf Coast University, 2022.

Stewart, Laura, and Susanne Hupp. *Historic Homes of Florida*. Pineapple Press, 2008.

Strauss, Elissa. "The Uncomfortable Truth in *The Giving Tree*." *The Week*, January 10, 2015.

Tampa Bay Times. "Salvage Finds More Than Cargo." September 3, 2005.

Tarnowski, Marilyn. "Shipwreck Museum May Lose Its Lease," *Key West Citizen*, August 13, 1992.

Taylor, Gary. "Killer Tied to '89 Death: Wife Suspected Him All Along." *Orlando Sentinel*, October 23, 2018.

Thiesen, William. "The Long Blue Line: Barbara Mabrity, Long-Time Lighthouse Keeper and Hurricane Hero." United States Coast Guard, March 26, 2021. https://www.mycg.uscg.mil.

Toppino, Nancy. *Insider's Guide to the Florida Keys and Key West*. Falcon Publishing, 2000.

Turrell, Todd T., Brian C. Schmitt, and Robert S. Carr. *The Florida Keys: A History Through Maps*. Island Map Publishing, n.d.

Twine, Charlotte. "The Past Lives On: The Old Key West Jail Will Be a Museum." *Keys Weekly*, May 25, 2021.

Vaizey, Marina. "Public Sculpture." *RSA Journal* 140, no. 5432 (August 1, 1992): 626.

Viele, John. *Tales of Yesterday's Florida Keys*. Pineapple Press, 2017.

Villoch, Margarita. "Key West's San Carlos." ActiveRain, November 15, 2012. https://activerain.com.

Walton, Emily. "Plant Ramble in April at West Martello Tower," *Key West Citizen*, January 16, 1987.

Watson, Keri. *Florida's New Deal Parks and Post Office Murals*. The History Press, 2024.

White, Ellen. *Key West: Paradise Found*. Pineapple Press, 2024.

Wilkinson, Jerry. "Historical Chronological Time Line." Keys Historeum. https://keyshistory.org/chronos.html.

Williams, Betty. "It's Official: The Joe Allen Garden Center." *Key West Citizen*, September 16, 1984.

Williams, Joy. *The Florida Keys: A History & Guide*. Random House, 1987.

Willis, J.A. *The New and Greater Key West Florida Told in Picture and Story.* Key West Board of Trade, 1914.

Woods, Amy. "Haunted House Owners Enjoying Their Friendly Ghost." *Key West Citizen*, October 30, 1989.

Wright, Andy. "The Story Behind the World's Most Terrifying Doll." Atlas Obscura, October 21, 2021.

Wright, Lynne E. *Disasters and Heroic Rescues*. Morris Book Publishing, 2006.

Zombek, Angie. "A Silent Threat: Key West, Yellow Fever, and Union Volunteers, 1861–1862." National Museum of Civil War Medicine, October 22, 2018.

Bob and Liz Randall at the end of the line.

About the Authors

Bob and Liz are a husband-and-wife photojournalist team. *Haunted Florida Keys* is their seventh book about Florida history. They live in Lake Mary, Florida.

Other nonfiction books by Liz and Bob Randall include:

Haunted St. Augustine and St. Johns County
Women in White: The Haunting of Northeast Florida
Murder in St. Augustine: The Mysterious Death of Athalia Ponsell Lindsley
An Ocklawaha River Odyssey
Past and Present: Historic Orlando
Secret St. Augustine

Contact Liz and Bob at https://www.elizabethrandallauthor.com.

Visit us at
www.historypress.com